CATHOLICISM IN ENGLISH-SPEAKING LANDS
IS VOLUME
92
OF THE
Twentieth Century Encyclopedia of Catholicism
UNDER SECTION
IX
THE CHURCH AND THE MODERN WORLD
IT IS ALSO THE
116TH
VOLUME IN ORDER OF PUBLICATION

Edited by **HENRI DANIEL-ROPS** *of the Académie Française*

CATHOLICISM
IN ENGLISH-SPEAKING
LANDS

By *M. P. CARTHY, O.S.U.*

HAWTHORN BOOKS · PUBLISHERS · *New York*

First Edition, February, 1964

NIHIL OBSTAT

Daniel Duivesteijn, S.T.D.

Censor Deputatus

IMPRIMATUR

☒ Georgius L. Craven

Episcopus Sebastopolis, Vicarius Generalis

Westmonasterii, die XXIII DECEMBRIS MCMLXIII

53645 -

CONTENTS

To

The Right Reverend John Tracy Ellis
Professor of Church History
in
The Catholic University of America
to whom this work owes
any merit it may possess.

CHAPTER I

FOUNDATIONS

Catholics in English-speaking countries today number some 61,000,000; they are under the spiritual care of more than 500 bishops and over 88,000 priests, not to mention the approximately 300,000 men and women members of the numerous religious Orders and Congregations and the steadily mounting number of Catholic schools and charitable institutions. In one brief narrative it is obviously impossible to undertake a well-rounded account of all aspects of Catholicism, even of all the significant ones, in such widely differing lands as England, Scotland, Wales, Ireland, the United States, Canada, Australia, New Zealand, and South Africa. But there may be an advantage in attempting to bring together some of the more important details relating to the beginnings of the Church and the development of its institutions and traditions in these different parts of the English-speaking world, and to point out the extent to which they either are features of a common pattern or differ from that pattern. For while all of English Catholicism is clearly in the historic stream of the faith, it ineluctably developed distinctive characteristics as it dealt with the challenges presented in the various countries to which it spread. Apart from a few injudicious generalizations regarding the peculiarly Irish character of Catholicism in English-speaking lands with its clergy-dominated, liturgy-resisting, and anti-intellectual qualities, little attention has been given to this subject. Despite the bond of common language, British and American coreligionists generally have shown only limited comprehension of the

similarities and differences which mark their religious heritage. While cursory reasons can be adduced to explain this
phenomenon, it must also be remembered that even close
cousins frequently need to be introduced to each other.

BRITAIN AND IRELAND

Christianity first came to Britain with the Romans but the
departure of the legions in 428 delivered up the land to the
fierce paganism of the Anglo-Saxon invaders, forcing the
Church to retreat to the Celtic fringe of the British Isles. During the haphazard colonization and settlement of Britain by
these Teutonic conquerors which occupied about 150 years,
a period longer than was required for the winning of the West
by Americans, Christianity survived in Wales where the
Church maintained its succession of priests and bishops. Unfortunately, these held themselves so severely aloof from
their barbarian foes, the English, that the task of bringing
the faith back to England was delayed until the end of the
sixth century when it was accomplished from two other
sources, Ireland and Rome.

Unlike Britain, Ireland was never part of the Roman Empire, but relations with Britain and the continent of Europe
account for the introduction of Christianity into Ireland before
the fifth century. From about 432 on, however, the whole of
Christian history in its Irish origins was destined to be closely
linked to the work of a single man. Despite the beguiling
number of theories offered by modern Patrician scholarship
concerning St Patrick's birthplace, his chronology, and even
how many there were of him, there seems to be no compell-
ing reason for abandoning the substance of older Patrician
tradition in these matters. The son of a Roman-British family,
Magonus Sucatus Patricius, or Patrick as the world now re-
members him, was captured by Irish pirates about A.D. 400,
taken to Antrim and sold as a slave to Miluic, a local chief-
tain. After six years of captivity he escaped from Ireland,
studied to be a monk under St Germanus of Auxerre, and

returned to Ireland as a missionary bishop in 432 to spend the rest of his life working for the conversion of the people "at the world's rim". A century or so later, in 563, the missionary Columba, or Colmcille as he was called in Irish, left Ireland and founded the monastery of Iona which became one of the most important of Irish missionary churches. From it Columba and his disciples evangelized Scotland, and from it went forth the mission which brought Christianity back to England.

In the same year as Columba died, 597, St Gregory the Great sent the Roman missionary Augustine to convert the pagan Anglo-Saxons. But progress was so slow that after nearly forty years of zealous effort the mission was still confined to Kent, and even in that small kingdom there was little guarantee of permanency. In 635, however, when Oswald, who as an exile had been educated at Iona, recovered his kingdom of Northumbria, which included northern England and a good part of southern Scotland, he appealed to Iona for help. According to Venerable Bede, one of the leading European historians of the day,

> They gladly assented and sent him a bishop named Aidan . . . Now when the bishop came to the King he assigned him a place and an episcopal residence in Lindisfarne, in accordance with his own prayer and desire . . . and oft there was the fair spectacle, when the bishop was teaching the word of God, that as he was not quite familiar with English, the King himself, being fully acquainted with the Irish tongue, acted as an interpreter of the heavenly doctrine . . . At that time many came daily from the land of the Irish into Britain and with great fervour preached and taught Christ's faith. . . .

It was from this little island of Lindisfarne of Aidan and his successors that Christian life was diffused over all the Northumbrian realm, and later over the great midland district of England, and ultimately to the territory of the East Saxons. While there may be some exaggeration in the statement that "Augustine was the apostle of Kent; Aidan was the apostle of England," there is nevertheless a sense in which it is true to say that St Aidan holds the first place in the evangelization of the English people. Certainly, Irish activity was responsible for the conversion of the midlands and of the east, while its influence was felt even towards the south, in Wessex, all of which was important in preparing the way for the work of Theodore of Tarsus who arrived in England in 669 as Archbishop of Canterbury. It was he who first divided up the dioceses with some degree of adequacy and gave England a hierarchical system that transcended State and racial boundaries, at the same time strengthening the bonds that already united that country to the See of Rome. By the close of the Anglo-Saxon period some seventeen bishoprics had been founded or refounded including such renowned ones as Canterbury, London, York, Lindisfarne or Durham, as well as others which became famous later under the names of Sarum, Lincoln, Norwich, and Exeter.

Despite the adaptability of the ancient monastic organization associated with the early Christianization of Britain, it proved incapable of providing permanently for the spiritual needs of a Christian population. With the passing of time, then, this monastic framework gradually gave way to a parochial system under which it was the oratory of the local lord which became the parish church, and his private chaplain who was transformed into the parish priest. In this way the great landowner became the *patronus ecclesiae,* asserting the right to present for ordination any cleric of his own choice. In time a similar right was claimed by temporal sovereigns in regard to episcopal consecration on the ground that the king was the lord of all the lands from which the bishop derived his revenues. So widespread were the abuses of this system that many of the most important sees of Western Christendom were occupied by licentious and corrupt men who more often than not had obtained their promotion by payment of money or by simoniacal compacts. It is not surprising that under such ecclesiastical superiors, the rank and file of the clergy degenerated in an equal if not greater degree. In England, the calamities of the Danish incursions

exercised a further disastrous effect upon the life of the
Church with the consequence that even the repeated efforts
of such men as St Dunstan of Canterbury and the saintly
King Edward the Confessor accomplished little in the way of
reform. However, by 1066, the year of St Edward's death,
forces which were to purify and renew the Church were already at work. Under Pope Leo IX and his counsellor Hilde-
brand, who later became Gregory VII, effective action was
at last initiated to restrain clerical incontinence and avarice
and to free the Church from the incubus of investiture.

THE NORMAN CONQUEST AND AFTER

With the arrival of William the Conqueror in 1066, England was to experience a period of strong kingship, clearer
laws and stricter discipline, with results that were undoubtedly beneficial to the Church. The systematic reforms
introduced by William and his archbishop, Lanfranc of Canterbury, provided the country with good bishops and thus
the struggle over investiture developed somewhat later in
England than on the continent. With the death of Lanfranc,
however, evil times fell upon the English Church so that it
was under the scholarly and saintly Anselm of Bec who in
1093 succeeded to the metropolitan See of Canterbury, that
the investiture struggle reached an acute phase. Largely as a
result of the resolute stand taken by St Anselm and the Holy
See, an agreement was reached in 1107 whereby the King
renounced his claims to investiture although the oath of fealty
was still exacted. This settlement ended a struggle which,
ecclesiastically speaking, was probably more momentous
than any other event in history down to the time of the Reformation.

Inevitably, however, the triumph of the Church in the
investiture strife had its unfortunate consequences in the so-
called secularization of the medieval Church against which
there soon arose new ascetic and reforming movements which
aimed at, and partly succeeded in monachizing the Church

by putting before the clergy, and even the laity, monastic discipline and monastic practices and ideals as the universal way of salvation. The renewing effects of the work of such groups as the Austin Canons, the Cistercians, and the Carthusians began to be felt in England in the first half of the twelfth century and were carried forward in the thirteenth century by the Dominicans and Franciscans who arrived there in 1221 and 1224 respectively.

But despite these and other efforts, the late Middle Ages were marked by a rapid and catastrophic decline of the papacy. The Avignon period was followed by the great Schism of the West from which the Church was delivered only by an ecumenical Council held in Constance from 1414-18. Although the Council succeeded in bringing about a return of the popes to Rome, the lack of unanimity concerning the measures to be taken against the many abuses in the Church resulted in the defeat of any reform action. Under the Renaissance papacy, curial abuses increased, aggravating the already widespread discontent with Church officialdom. The spokesmen of radical reform included loyal churchmen such as Nicholas of Cusa, Vincent Ferrer, John Capistran, and others, as well as revolutionaries like Marsiglio of Padua in Italy and John Wycliffe in England. In the latter country, the rise and spread of Lollardy, the movement which grew out of Wycliffe's doctrines, profoundly disturbed English life during the latter part of the fourteenth century and for many years thereafter. It was perhaps all too typical of episcopal policy that Wycliffe's key doctrine on the importance of Scripture, his insistence that the sacred text should be translated into every man's own tongue since only then could men learn for themselves God's message to mankind, was answered only by an official ban and suppression of his erroneous version rather than by some move to produce a new Catholic version or to have the old version amended and printed. Thus in the thirteen years immediately preceding Martin Luther's thesis sheet of 1517, bishops' tribunals in England held no fewer than 365 processes for heresy, most of them involving religious opinions which were survivals from the Lollard movement. That the crisis of Lollardy was serious, no one can deny, but it was not the Lollards, not even the Hussites, nor Lutherans, nor Zwinglians who eventually produced an effective solvent of traditional English Catholicism. Rather it was the royal "Defender of the Faith," Henry VIII, whose successful defiance of the pope led to the withdrawal of his realm from the pope's authority. Before concerning ourselves with the story of the English Reformation, however, it will be useful to turn aside and briefly trace the pre-Reformation history of those parts of the British Isles outside England about which thus far we have made only incidental mention.

MEDIEVAL IRELAND, SCOTLAND AND WALES

As we have already noted, the predominantly pagan island to which St Patrick returned around 432 underwent such an astonishing transformation that at his death the Christian faith was widely accepted and fervently practised throughout Ireland. The next century saw an even more remarkable development: Irish missionaries leaving the land so recently converted in well nigh limitless numbers to evangelize not only Scotland and England but to establish centres of knowledge and piety in many parts of Europe where the barbarian invasions had all but extinguished Western culture. In this "Island of saints and scholars," the form of the medieval *Christianitas* differed somewhat from that which developed in Europe. Although always at one with Rome in fundamentals, the Irish Church deviated in small details such as the date of Easter and the form of the tonsure. In the temporal sphere, the Brehon law and not feudalism was the basis of secular administration, while in the field of religion ecclesiastical administration was based on the monastic and not the episcopal system. It was in the monasteries that Irish culture flowered most brilliantly and where the exquisite illumina-

tion of Irish manuscripts such as the *Book of Kells* equalled
the best work of its kind done anywhere in Europe. Irish
monks likewise made great progress in the study of Scripture,
canon law, and philosophy, and early Irish epic verse can be
said to have something of the vigor and vividness of Homer.
Nor were the accomplishments of women far behind those
of the men in this work of founding monasteries and schools,
as is evidenced by the lives of a St Monnine, St Brigid, St
Ira and others.

From the fifth to the twelfth centuries, the general history
of Ireland and that of Western Christendom developed along
parallel lines. The widespread decadence of the ninth and
tenth centuries was reflected in the Irish Church, while lack
of political unity exposed the island to invasions which
further weakened the Church. The defeat of the Northmen
at Clontarf in 1014 by the great Irish king, Brian Boru, put
a temporary stop to these invasions, while the inspiration of
the Gregorian reform movement was reflected in the remarkable work accomplished in Ireland under the great St
Malachy, Archbishop of Armagh. Many salutary reforms
were initiated, and the old monastic system was gradually
abolished and the country divided into regular dioceses ruled
by bishops. Scarcely had this been accomplished when in
1154 Adrian IV, the only Englishman who was ever elected
pope, granted Ireland to King Henry II, thereby opening it
to Norman or Anglo-Norman invaders. It was not, however,
until after his difficulties following the murder of Thomas
Becket that Henry himself showed any interest in the island.
Then, in 1171, hoping to escape from the embarrassments
of his crime by a foreign expedition, he led a force into Ireland where he received the submission of most of the Irish
chiefs. Although English kings thenceforth assumed the title
Lord of Ireland, until Henry VIII took the title of King of
Ireland, English rule long remained limited to an eastern
district called the Pale, near Dublin.

Ignored for the most part by medieval English kings, Ireland was left to the at times tempestuous management of its

Celtic chiefs and Norman barons. After the establishment of the native Irish hierarchy in 1152, a fairly clear line was drawn in practice between the authority of the Church which should be concerned with purely religious matters, and that of the kings and lords who competed among themselves for control of temporal society. Although not based on a theory of separation of Church and State which would have been unthinkable at the time, this practice of Irish churchmen in the twelfth century was based on a determined opposition to lay interference which soon became opposition to Norman and English interference, whether lay or ecclesiastical. The important consequences of this may well be reflected in the sixteenth-century Irish resistance to the might of the crown and Irish rejection of English heresy. It may also help to explain the great satisfaction which Irishmen felt at the independence of the Church and the State which they found existing in the settlements to which they flocked in the modern English-speaking world.

While a vague suzerainty over both Wales and Scotland was claimed by many English kings, none of them before Edward I did much to enforce their claims. Both countries, therefore, tended to remain more Celtic than England, although the many Scandinavian raids which Scotland suffered, in common with England and Ireland, resulted in a considerable Norse influence on Scottish life. The early history of Wales is part of the history of Imperial Rome while the end of the Roman occupation marked the beginning of Celtic monachism. Although Church discipline at first followed closely that of Rome, the Germanic invasion cut Wales off from direct communication with the rest of Christendom. The result was that not only did Welsh priests refuse to have anything to do with St Augustine when he arrived to evangelize the Anglo-Saxons, but they also sanctioned peculiar usages in ritual and discipline which were cherished as symbols of nationality. However, in the ninth century Wales renounced all such national customs as were held unorthodox by Rome and even accepted, though with some reluctance, the metropolitan jurisdiction of Canterbury. When the native Welsh dynasty came to an end in 1282 with the death of Llywelyn, the last prince, Edward I reorganized the Principality of Wales, naming his son Edward Prince of Wales, a title thereafter conferred on the eldest sons of English sovereigns. Though for a long time the Welsh regarded the English as alien conquerors, the country slowly entered into full partnership with England, and Wales remained devoutly Catholic and devotedly Roman until the accession to the English throne of the Welsh Tudor dynasty.

The monastery of Iona, founded as a mother house by Columba in 563, continued in fact to be the centre of Columban jurisdiction all during the monastic period of the Church in the country now known as Scotland, though that name did not come into use until the eleventh century. Early in the eighth century, the Columban monasteries fell into the hands of the then dominant Culdees who, together with the newly arrived secular clergy, carried on the work of evangelization begun at Iona. At the time of the Norman conquest of England, great evils afflicted the Scottish Church where the lack of a proper ecclesiastical government aggravated the abuses of lay interference in Church government and clerical concubinage then also rife in other parts of Christendom. The accession of Malcolm III in 1057 and his subsequent marriage to a Saxon noblewoman who had fled with her family to Scotland after the Battle of Hastings, marked a new era in the introduction of English ideas and English civilization into Scotland. Largely under the influence of this same Queen Margaret, reform of outstanding abuses in such matters as the Lenten fast, Easter communion, Sunday observance, and compliance with the Church's marriage laws was effected, thereby bringing the Scottish Church into line with the rest of Catholic Christendom. In the course of time, too, the diocesan form of Church government was established and the Culdees were gradually superseded by the regular monastic orders.

After securing the conquest of Wales, Edward I made

several attempts to carry out his plan of union with Scotland. When his invasion of Scotland in 1296 met with success, Edward made himself King of Scotland in his own name and right and caused the Stone of Scone, reputed to be the very pillar on which Jacob slept and had his vision of the angels, to be removed to England and placed in Westminster Abbey where it has remained ever since. But when the English and Scottish forces met again at Bannock Burn in 1314, the Scots' victory assured Scottish independence which was formally recognized by England in 1328 in the Treaty of Northampton. The kingdom, however, continued to be disturbed not only by border wars with the English, but also by the lawlessness of its own turbulent barons. These disturbances weakened the Scottish Church which was also called upon to take stern measures against the spread of Lollardism and in 1525 against the new heresy which reached Scotland in the Calvinistic rather than the Anglican form.

THE REFORMATION IN THE BRITISH ISLES

That Catholicism in the countries of the British Isles on the eve of Henry VIII's quarrel with Rome was not without its serious weaknesses is abundantly evident even from this cursory survey. Nevertheless, even after the grave internal abuses, not to mention the Wycliffe movement, the Schism of the West, and the humanist revival of learning had done their worst, the general tradition remained integrally Catholic. Certainly, the anti-clericalism, the weaknesses and abuses in the ecclesiastical system, and the various heresies already active in England were important factors in the sixteenth-century revolution that was to make the religion of that country royal and national rather than papal and Catholic. Despite Henry VIII's traditionalist and conservative views on Church doctrine and government it was through his quarrel with the pope on the question of his divorce from Catherine of Aragon that the English Reformation began. It was largely an insular process and was responsive to peculiar political and social forces. Henry VIII, on a last analysis, accomplished the over-throw of papal supremacy and carried out the dissolution of the monasteries, largely in pursuance of a policy of extending the sovereignty of the central government into all spheres of the national society. In Germany, Lutheranism began as a heresy and ended in schism, but the contrary was the case in England where the separation from Rome began as a schism and eventually developed into a heresy. Since the story of the Reformation is too long and involved for review here, it will be more important for our purposes simply to note its implications for the future history of English-speaking countries.

The anger and resentment against the papacy bred in Henry by the experiences of the marriage suit changed his friendship for popes into enmity, and alienated the only power which might have kept in check the anti-papal and anti-sacerdotal tendencies then growing up in England. It is almost unthinkable that the ruin of the Catholic Church in England could have been accomplished without the complicity of the government. But having once jettisoned the foundation principle of historical Christianity, Henry himself, regardless of his personal views, was powerless to set limits to the consequences of this rejection. The result, therefore, for the ordinary Englishman was to set a fashion, followed all too faithfully during the succeeding centuries, for a bitter hatred of nearly every feature of Catholic belief and practice, particularly the Mass, the Mother of God, and the papacy. The myths and misconceptions, the modes of thinking and acting which were initiated in the time of Henry and Elizabeth, and legalized in the various acts of supremacy, suppression, and uniformity, were thereafter strengthened by the unhappy inheritance of each succeeding generation. Protestantism in England, as John Henry Newman pointed out, came to be embodied in the person of the sovereign. As a religion grafted upon loyalty, its strength was "not in argument, not in fact, not in the unanswerable controversialist, not in apostolic succession, not in sanction of Scripture—

but in a royal road to faith, in backing up a king whom men see, against a pope whom they do not see." Hence in the logical and historical order the next step was to pass sweeping ecclesiastical legislation which exalted the crown above the Gospel and substituted "the lion and the dog" for the Cross. Priests were harried out of the country as traitors, and Protestantism was made the passport to office and authority. The oath was required not only of the king, his court, and both houses of Parliament, but also, by 1563, of all judges, lawyers, officers in the army and navy, members of the universities, and national clergy. With this tradition established in every function and department of the state, the English became a people who would *ex animo* swear to the truth of a religion which indulged their natural turn of mind and required no effort. So it was that the assumptions of the English Protestant tradition came to be "among the elements of knowledge, unchangeable as the moods of logic, or the idioms of language, or the injunctions of good taste, or the proprieties of good manners". As a consequence, Elizabeth's reign was forever enshrined as "golden," while Mary's must never be anything but "bloody". Inevitably "pope" and "pagan" became synonymous, as did also "the Pope, the Devil and the Pretender." This tradition of information, not authenticated but immemorial, took for granted that the Catholic Church was a "simple monster of iniquity".

As in England, so in Scotland, the aim of the reformers was to stamp out every outward vestige of the ancient faith. But the Scottish Reformation was not the work of kings. The short and decisive contest which resulted in the overthrow of the old religion and the establishment of the reform of John Calvin with a national kirk on the model of the Church of Geneva was largely the work of a group, small in numbers but strong in energy and conviction, under the leadership of John Knox. They were, it is true, immensely aided by the numerous and crying abuses which had for too long been rampant in the Scottish Church. Thus by 1560 conditions were ripe to put into effect that change in religion which the

Calvinists were resolved to have. Protestant feeling was predominant in the parliament that met in Edinburgh and with only the feeblest of protests from the bishops there present, the Calvinist confession of faith was set forth, papal jurisdiction was abolished, the saying or hearing of Mass was not only forbidden, but the offering of the holy Sacrifice was labelled idolatrous and made a capital offence.

The measures enacted by this assembly of the estates gave the Scottish people a religious settlement so strongly fashioned that it lasted as long as the Elizabethan settlement in England. Since resistance to the settlement was non-existent, there was in Scotland nothing like the long and persistent persecution that prevailed in England and took the lives of countless priests and layfolk. But the same hatred of Catholicism became a national obsession in Scotland where it was aggravated by the fierce political struggle associated with the unhappy Mary Stuart who in the end was dethroned and forced to flee to England, only to fall into the hands that had successfully backed the Protestant forces in Scotland. Such Catholics as remained in Scotland were driven into hiding, forming a negligible minority, not to be taken into account. The kirk became the pillar of Scotland's new faith as nobles, scholars, and peasants all subscribed to the Presbyterian confession of faith. Moreover, it was this faith of Calvin and Knox that Scotsmen carried far and wide, and with it went also the bitter anti-Catholic animus of the mother country.

The destruction of the old religion in Wales was the work of Englishmen exclusively. As a foreign importation, the new faith was imposed by the sheer might of English officialdom. Although the Welsh were a Catholic people and an independent people, Henry VIII succeeded in making Wales a province of England, thereby bringing its people under the laws of England, and its clergy under the supremacy of the crown. When he decreed the dissolution of the monasteries in 1536, the resultant impoverishment of the country was far graver than that in England or Scotland. In losing the monks and friars, the Welsh were deprived not only of spirit-

ual guides but also of their prime patrons of the arts, tillers
of the soil, and educators of the poor. However lacking in
spiritual vigour the monasteries of the times were, they remained nevertheless the patrons of the bards and an integral
element of the prevailing social organization. Now, however,
the entire structure of society crumbled at the same time that
a grim era of religious persecution was inaugurated.

How little the new doctrines appealed to the Welsh people was evidenced during the Marian restoration when only
three men were burnt for heresy in Wales, and not one of
them was a Welshman. As late as 1580, Catholicism was
admittedly still the faith of the majority of the Welsh people.
However, as the old priests of Mary's reign passed away and
their places were left unfilled, the extinction of the old religion was inevitable. The Anglican, that is, the State Church,
remained the Elizabethan settlement which tried to force the
English language on a people who preferred their native
tongue. Save for the hunted priests who came and went, ministering to the dwindling group of Catholics, there was no
one for 200 years to tend the spiritual wants of the spiritually
starved Welsh people who, losing even the Christian faith,
turned to memories of pre-Christian worship and clung to
superstitions of pagan origin. Not until the eighteenth century, as we shall see later, was a new religious response
elicited from the country at large, and then it was a Calvinistic Methodism that captured the hearts of the Welsh people.

In Ireland the progress of events was quite otherwise. At
the time that Henry VIII led England into schism, Ireland,
though nominally subject to the English crown since the
reign of Henry II and partly colonized by English and Norman knights, was little affected by English rule or Anglo-
Norman influence. Within the English Pale which comprised
the counties of Dublin, Louth, Meath, Westmeath, and
Kildare, and in which there were traces of English organization, the Henrician schism caused some religious confusion. But it made very little impression in the rest of the country where in 1537, the Irish looked upon the new heresy

as merely another in a long series of objectionable moves by an alien power. Later English efforts to impose the new religion in Ireland by law and to "abolish idolatry, papistry, the Mass sacrament and the like" likewise met with little success. Instead, clergy and faithful alike were more solidly confirmed in their commitment to the Christian faith and their allegiance to the See of Peter.

AFTERMATH OF THE REFORMATION

Under Elizabeth, repression of papists began in earnest, and during her long reign a series of insurrections under Shane O'Neill, Earl of Tyrone, and his successor Hugh O'Neill, kept English armies busy in Ireland. Efforts were made to "plant" the island with English settlers on lands forfeited by rebellion, but none of these Elizabethan plantations survived as discernible units beyond the queen's reign. At her death, however, most of the monastic and conventual institutions which had continued to flourish notwithstanding legal suppression had been effectively closed. Oppression of papists continued with varying intensity during the seventeenth century. Under Oliver Cromwell and the Puritan régime, the subjugation of Ireland was accomplished with such violence that for years to come 'the curse of Cromwell' was the most bitter of Irish oaths. In 1653 Ireland and Scotland were incorporated with England into a single centralized Commonwealth, but the fact that the union rested on force did not recommend it to the majority of Irishmen or Scotsmen.

Real damage was done to the Church in Ireland during this period which was the era of the hedge-school and the Mass-rock, as well as one which produced uncounted martyrs for the faith. The republican interlude in English history was ended in 1660 by the Stuart Restoration. Under Charles II measures were passed which drove thousands of Puritans into exile in the American colonies and did nothing to improve the lot of Irish Catholics who looked in vain for some show of

Stuart gratitude for their services in bringing about the restoration. Nevertheless, the Irish continued to support James
II, who had succeeded his brother Charles in 1685, when he
fled from England in 1688 leaving the English throne to
William of Orange whom the Protestants had invited over
from Holland. Two years later, however, William's victory
at the Battle of the Boyne ended the war and Protestant ascendancy was again secured.

In England, William's Toleration Act of 1689 granted
religious liberty, though not religious equality, to dissenters,
but did not apply to Roman Catholics. In practice, however,
this concession was interpreted widely enough so that even
Catholics were not molested throughout the country. Although William promised an extension of religious liberty
to Ireland, that unhappy country remained an exception in
this matter, as in so many others. The Irish Parliament, representing only the Protestant minority, not only continued in
force the penal laws against Catholics, but embarked on new
discriminatory legislation. Under these laws, Catholics
were excluded from Parliament, from the bench and bar,
from the army and navy, and from all civil offices. Denied
their own schools at home, they were forbidden to attend
foreign schools, or inherit landed property, or hold land
under lease, or have arms or ammunition, or even a horse
worth five pounds. Only secular priests could remain in the
island and these must be registered; their churches could
have neither steeple nor bell. Catholic holidays were proscribed, as were pilgrimages, while inheritance and other
laws favoured those members of a family who turned Protestant.

Despite this long-sustained and ruthless effort to eradicate
the Catholic faith and replace it by the Christianity of the
Reformers which the English Crown had made its own, the
Irish continued to cling to the old religion. Generations of
priests returned in secrecy to Ireland after being trained and
ordained abroad and spent the rest of their lives preaching
and teaching, knowing that poverty would be their portion,

if not prison and the scaffold. Thus Protestantism made no progress and Catholicism more than held its own. But the steady pressure of the penal code did succeed in so impoverishing, debasing, and degrading Catholics as to leave them incapable of rebellion, if not ignorant of their wrongs. Edmund Burke, in describing the "vicious perfection" of this penal system wrote:

> I must do it justice: it was a complete system, full of coherence and consistency, well digested and well composed in all its parts. It was a machine of wise and elaborate contrivance, and as well fitted for the oppression, impoverishment, and degradation of a people, and the debasement, in them, of human nature itself as ever proceeded from the perverted ingenuity of man.

A few, with the connivance of friendly Protestants, managed to retain their estates, but the large majority sank to the level of cottiers and day-labourers, living always in the shadow of starvation. Excluded from every position of influence, rackrented by absentee landlords, forced to pay tithes to a Church they abhorred, and hating the government which oppressed them, many of the more ambitious quitted the land of their birth to find employment in the armies of Europe and later, as we shall see, even beyond the Atlantic.

Relaxation of the penal laws did not come until the close of the eighteenth century when grudging concessions began to be made. During all these centuries, the Irish remained constant in the faith and true to Rome. The population of the island had increased—from about 1,250,000 in 1700 to about 4,500,000 in 1800—and of the latter more than two-thirds were Catholic. But the long centuries of the Protestant ascendancy with its persecution and social and cultural depression and belittlement inevitably left their mark not only on Ireland, but on the Irish, with the result that from them came no major contributions to the intellectual or devotional life of the Church. Nevertheless, their long history of fidelity did blossom into a national missionary vocation that inspired thousands of Irish priests and Irish emigrants to carry the light of the faith to the four corners of the globe, and to play a large part in the growth and character of the Church in the United States, Canada, Australia, New Zealand, and South Africa, to which we shall now turn our attention.

DEVELOPMENTS IN ENGLISH AMERICA AND CANADA

Although the penal codes of England were not *ipso facto* applicable to her American colonies, the animus against Catholics was brought to Jamestown in 1607 and found ready expression in colonial charters and legislation which made the Catholic faith an illegal religion and its practice a crime. In English America, as in the home country, Catholics were an outlawed race—in practice of their religion, in education of their children, in ownership of property, in exercise of franchise, in exclusion from the militia and offices of distinction, and in general ostracism from the social, civil, and political life of the community. The Catholic clergy, too, were the objects of special legislation patterned on that of the home country. When Maryland was founded in 1634 by Lord Baltimore, it not only provided a refuge for the Calverts' Catholic brethren, but it also offered the hope that for the first time in history all Christian sects could live together peaceably, possessing equal rights. But this daring experiment in religious freedom was short-lived. An increase in the number of Puritan inhabitants resulted in the overthrow of the proprietor's government, and the ensuing régime, in October 1654, repealed the famous Act of Toleration of 1649 and outlawed the "popish" religion.

During the eighteenth century, Catholics were not only excluded from much of the social and political life of the community, they were also the object of laws aimed at complete suppression of Catholic worship. When Queen Anne, more tolerant than her American subjects, refused royal assent to some of these laws, and insisted that priests be per-

mitted to exercise their functions in private, the practice
arose, as in England, of erecting chapels or "Priests' Mass
Houses" in connection with the manor houses of the wealth-
ier Catholics of the community. From the earliest days the
spiritual needs of the American colonists were cared for by
the Jesuit Fathers whose lot, however, was not an enviable
one. Nevertheless, Fathers Andrew White and John Altham,
who were members of the original Maryland expedition, as
well as their later confrères and successors worked on. When
freedom dawned for the colonists, they were the only clerical body in the new republic.

Pennsylvania and New York were the only other colonies
with Catholic populations large enough to be counted, and
even there the temper of the times was often so bitterly anti-
Catholic as to keep the numbers from increasing. The first
law establishing religious liberty in New York was that of
1683 enacted by the Catholic governor, Thomas Dongan,
but with the fall of James II in England, drastic penal laws
against Catholics came into operation here as elsewhere in
the English-speaking world. That few Catholics had the
temerity to establish themselves in New England gives no
cause for wonder. The Puritans of sixteenth- and seven-
teenth-century England were by far the bitterest persecutors
of Catholics, and their spiritual descendants in the new world
who formed the majority in Connecticut and Massachusetts
Bay, and whose ideas found acceptance in Plymouth, New
Hampshire, and Maine, may well claim the same distinction.

There is no lack of evidence, then, that the bitter hostility
towards Catholicism fostered in England after the middle of
the sixteenth century was transmitted intact to America where
it found expression in every aspect of colonial life. While
English Protestants brought their prejudices with them to the
new world, English Catholic emigrants in their turn were
not devoid of the heritage of degradation which had accus-
tomed them to accept the condition of pariahs. Their acute
awareness of the Protestant animus restrained them from
attempting to establish relations with other groups and led

many to resign themselves to their own inferiority. Only with the advent of the American Revolution was a movement initiated which, on the one side, marked the first weakening of the deeply ingrained prejudices of American Protestants, and on the other, modified the traditional Catholic instinct towards isolation.

In Canada, the Roman Catholic Church dates its beginnings from the early seventeenth century when under French rule Jesuits, Franciscan Recollects, and Sulpicians ministered to the needs of the French colonists and worked for the conversion of the Indians. The Ursulines, founded in 1535 for the education of young women, were outstanding as an early channel for the participation of women in the making of Canada. When Great Britain acquired Canada in 1763 under the Treaty of Paris, there were about 65,000 French Catholics distributed among the towns of Quebec, Three Rivers, and Montreal, with well-organized parishes along the banks of the St Lawrence, all served by some 196 priests and six Orders of women. Because of the unrest in the thirteen colonies, the English deemed it wise not to add a dissatisfied French Canada to the forces then menacing British rule in America. Thus, in contrast with the disabilities under which English Catholics at home and in the colonies laboured, the British government granted concessions to their newly acquired Canadian Catholic subjects. Although the American colonists as yet had no Anglican bishop in their midst, the Canadians were permitted to receive Jean Olivier Briand, who had been consecrated in Paris in 1766, for the see of Quebec. During his episcopate, the Quebec Act was passed in 1774 reestablishing French law and restoring to the Canadians their most precious civil and religious liberties. Prompted chiefly by the desire to hold the loyalty of the French in face of the growing revolt in the thirteen colonies, the Act did in fact keep Canada from taking part in the American Revolution which issued in the independence of the United States. As a result of that struggle, many loyalists, determined to maintain their British allegiance, moved to Canada, establishing themselves at the outset chiefly in Quebec and Montreal. Problems soon arose from the demands of these loyalists for better educational facilities and for the establishment of English as the sole language superseding French. These were partially resolved by the Constitutional Act of 1791 which divided the country into Upper Canada where English law and customs were standard, and Lower Canada where French customs and practices continued with the addition of representative institutions.

Unlike the first American colonies, the two outposts of Western Christendom, Australia and New Zealand, were later developments which were not initially established from deeply religious motives or with a strong missionary purpose. Treatment of them here will therefore be relatively brief since our main concern in this chapter is with pre-nineteenth century developments.

AUSTRALIA AND NEW ZEALAND

When the American Revolution closed the trans-Atlantic colonies as a compulsory dumping ground for the undesirable elements of the British Isles, the government seized upon the idea of using Australia to relieve the country's overcrowded prisons. Beginning in 1788, the main convict settlements were founded in or near Sydney, soon to become and to remain the leading city of Australia. In these early years, however, the wretched state of the little colony offered slight justification for the remark made by a French observer that the English had compensated themselves for the loss of one empire—the American—by gaining another, Australia. To be sure, not all who were deported to Australia were hardened criminals—many were merely victims of the great social changes which were transforming English life at the close of the eighteenth century. They included the destitute who defied the law in order to eat, and workers who agitated for social justice. The majority of the Irish convicted and transported to New South Wales were political reformers. Begun in 1791, the transportation from Ireland was greatly increased after the rebellion of 1798.

Conscious of the injustice done to them, these Irish political prisoners were further embittered by the degrading system to which they were submitted. The majority of the Irish were, of course, Catholics who were denied the ministration of a priest and forced to practise their faith in secret. An Ossory priest, James Walsh, had requested permission to accompany the first settlers, but to no avail. Among those transported for the rebellion of 1798 were three priests, Fathers James Harold, James Dixon, and Peter O'Neill, but they were forbidden to exercise their ministry. Not until 1803 when Father Dixon was conditionally emancipated was he allowed to act as chaplain in response to the repeated requests of the Catholics who then formed one-third of the population. After his return to Ireland in 1808, the Catholic population of Sydney remained without the services of a priest until the arrival in 1817 of the Irish missionary, Jeremiah O'Flynn. This intrepid priest not only brought spiritual solace to the abandoned Catholics of New South Wales during his brief stay, but he unwittingly precipitated a political crisis in England which won freedom of conscience and official recognition for the Catholic Church in Australia nine years before the coming of Catholic Emancipation in England.

When in 1840, Great Britain extended its reluctant protection to New Zealand, the number of Catholic colonists was about 500 in a total population of some 5,000. Until the arrival of its first vicar apostolic, Jean Baptiste François Pompallier, in 1838, accompanied by a group of the recently founded Marists, the colony was without the services of a priest. Systematic European settlement which began in 1840, after the growth of religious tolerance in the British Isles, left New Zealand relatively free of the convict element which had loomed so large in the early settlement of Australia, and of refugees from religious persecution such as had marked the history of the Thirteen Colonies. From the beginning,

missions were undertaken to the Maori aborigines, a Poly-
nesian people of vigorous, warlike character, skilled in many
arts and crafts. As in the case of the American Iroquois or
Sioux, however, fierce contests over land ensued between
the Maoris and the white settlers. Despite this warfare, the
Church made steady progress through the nineteenth century particularly, as we shall see later, under the leadership
of the Marists and the Mill Hill Fathers.

BRITISH SOUTH AFRICA

Finally, Catholic beginnings in British South Africa can be
pieced together in very brief fashion. Although Catholicism
had been introduced in the sixteenth century by the Portu-
guese, the Dutch rulers of the Cape colony during the seventeenth and eighteenth centuries had proscribed the Catholic
religion. When British possession of Cape Town was confirmed after the fall of Napoleon's empire in 1814, the initiative of the vicar apostolic of the London District, Bishop
William Poynter, led to the appointment of a Benedictine
bishop, Dom Bede Slater, as vicar apostolic of the Cape. But
the British government would not permit him to go there,
although beginning in 1820 they did allow a priest to act as
chaplain to the scattered Catholics of the area. Not until
1837, with the appointment of another Benedictine, Dom
Placid Morris, as vicar apostolic, does the real history of the
Church in South Africa begin.

CHAPTER II

EMANCIPATION AND NINETEENTH-CENTURY DEVELOPMENTS

ENGLAND

Catholicism in England was virtually moribund when, towards the close of the eighteenth century, the severity of the laws against it was first tempered. During the long night of Catholic decline, the well-laid plans of Elizabeth, Cecil and their successors had reduced the faithful to a mere handful almost completely broken in spirit. That Catholic England survived at all was due in large part to the success of William Allen's Douay movement which, beginning in 1568, produced a total of forty-four educational houses in various parts of Europe. These English colleges, particularly those at Douay and Rome, supplied the majority of the English secular clergy who, together with the scores of Jesuits and other religious who gave their lives to the English mission, helped to stiffen the resistance of loyal Catholics in their defiance of the architects of the system of 1559. But without an episcopate, it was inevitable that ecclesiastical organization and government in the country should suffer. As the soul of the Douay movement, William Allen, later cardinal, was designated prefect of the mission in 1581, and he remained the acknowledged leader of the English Catholics until his death in 1594.

The rule of archpriests without episcopal character which

lasted from 1598 to 1621 was an unfortunate period of almost complete paralysis. The Jesuit, Robert Persons, in his
Plan of 1597 called attention to the need for bishops to administer the sacraments of confirmation and holy orders, as
well as to give counsel and make decisions in the burning
religious questions of the day. But not until 1623 was the
first vicar apostolic appointed. It was this kind of government
which lasted until 1850, although the period from 1631 to
1685 was complicated by the fact that the sole vicar apostolic
was not resident in England. In 1688 under James II, England was divided into four districts and a vicar apostolic appointed for each. This structure remained until 1840 when
the four vicariates were increased to eight. But the long-stand-
ing hostility between an influential section of the secular
clergy and the Jesuits (later the regular clergy generally)
continued to bedevil the problem of Church government, a
heritage which the English Church has not altogether over-
come even today. Additional difficulties arose from the fact
that there were no parishes, no fixed missionary districts, no
chapels. Most of the clergy acted as family chaplains of the
Catholic gentry, with the natural sequel that often it was to
his patron rather than to his ecclesiastical superior that the
chaplain looked for authority. The result was a curious independence of both clerics and laity in their relations with
the vicars apostolic, an anomaly found later in other English-speaking countries.

So well did the British penal code succeed, that the Catholic group had shrunk by 1780 to what Edmund Burke
described as "but a handful of people (enough to torment
but not enough to fear), perhaps not so many, of both sexes
and of all ages, as fifty thousand". Moreover, their position
under the penal laws which, even when not actually enforced,
were always enforceable at a moment's notice, was so haz-
ardous and insecure as to breed in them a tradition of caution
and concealment which found expression in every aspect of
living. While isolation from the life of the nation was almost
inevitable during these years when profession of the faith

was so disadvantageous to worldly prospects, it was unfortunate that this enforced and accepted isolation was perpetuated long after the triumph of Catholic emancipation.

It is significant that the first measure of Catholic relief, in 1774, was in favour of Ireland, to be followed in 1778 by a further act which relieved English Catholics of some of the worst disabilities of former penal legislation but which was passed, not from motives of policy or humanity, but of sheer political necessity. At war with the American colonies and threatened by France and Spain, the English government courted the support of Catholics. Emboldened by the success of Catholics in Ireland, some members of the English Catholic aristocracy were stimulated into a timid assertion of their own claims to justice. Their petition to the king won for them more than the Irish Catholics had gained after twenty years of organized effort. When a proposal was made to extend the measure to Scotland, it was quickly withdrawn when it met with fierce Presbyterian opposition. It was not long before a general revival of anti-Catholic feeling erupted in the fearful Gordon Riots which convulsed the city of London in June, 1780. These demonstrations served to confirm the traditional Catholic fear of public action and undoubtedly helped to increase episcopal caution, thereby leaving the movement towards further relief largely to lay initiative.

When the Relief Act of 1791 containing a new oath of allegiance was being negotiated, the resultant controversy was not between the heirs of the Reformation and the descendants of those whom they had dispossessed, but rather a dispute between some of the Catholic laity to whose initiative the Act was due, and their ecclesiastical superiors, the Catholic bishops. Fearing that episcopal prerogative was being usurped, a group of bishops led by Charles Walmesley, Bishop of Rama and senior vicar apostolic in the Kingdom of England, censured the activity of the lay committee, pointing out that it was the province of bishops "to determine on the lawfulness of Oaths, Declarations, or other Instruments whatsoever containing Doctrinal matters". War was on between the bishops and the committee when the latter, in the forthright language of the day, justified their right "to call in question the irrefragability of your articles and determinations without incurring the guilt of heresy, schism or disobedience". This stormy controversy touched ultimately on the extent of the bishops' authority in matters touching politics in relation to religion.

This is no place to relate the history of the activities of the Catholic Committee and its work, after obtaining the Catholic Relief Acts, for Catholic Emancipation. The whole story is excessively complex and tangled. But it is worth noting that if the Committee's attitude was imbued with a species of Anglo-Gallicanism, and was nationalist even in religion and disposed to restrict papal authority and limit its interference, this was no novelty devised by disloyalty or schism or heresy (with all of which the Committee was charged). As E. I. Watkin has pointed out, it was in fact,

> the expression, indeed the final expression, of an attitude traditional in English Catholicism, represented by the Chapter's protest in 1685 against vicars apostolic and reaching back through the Elizabethan Appellants to the prereformation Church. The Committee was in fact historically justified in its later appeal to the fourteenth-century statutes of Provisors and Praemunire. What was novel was that Anglo-Gallicanism was now predominantly a layman's attitude, often with an anticlerical colour. . . . (*Roman Catholicism in England, from the Reformation to 1950*, p. 131).

Charles Butler (1750-1832), the nephew of Alban Butler, was the secretary of the Committee. He was a lawyer by profession—he could not practise until after the passage of the Relief Act of 1791—who did much for the Church in England despite the opposition of some of the vicars apostolic such as Milner, who did not scruple to write of him, "whenever any mischief to religion happens . . . I cannot help thinking that Charles Butler has a share in the business". But that was not the only time that Butler was slandered by Milner.

Meanwhile, the storm of the French Revolution had burst in all its fury, bringing many French clerical and lay refugees to England. This influx undoubtedly contributed to the general strength of the Catholic body, and although the majority returned home after Napoleon's concordat with the Holy See in 1801, some of them and their descendants attained to positions of considerable influence in England. The Revolution also necessitated the return to English soil of approximately forty English schools, colleges, seminaries, and convents which for so long had been scattered over France and the rest of Europe. Thus when the first stirrings of that intellectual revolution known as the Oxford Movement began to be felt in the Church a half century later, such institutions as Stonyhurst, Ushaw, St Edmund's (Old Hall), Oscott, Downside, and Ampleforth were already strongly entrenched and beginning to impinge on public consciousness.

With Catholic life resuming something of its former quiet tempo, it is not surprising that the cause of emancipation was becalmed. While some among the English laity were ambitious to carry forward the movement for total emancipation, no active leader appeared to give unity and purpose to the struggle. Moreover, various other national circumstances such as the acute economic and social distress resulting from the revolutions in agriculture, industry, and trade, as well as the growing demand for long-overdue political reform, all contributed to this delay. It was, therefore, more or less inevitable that control of the crusade for emancipation should have passed into the hands of the Irish.

Despite the legislative union between the two countries, the only thing the English and Irish Catholics had in common was their faith. To the Irish Catholic, the clergy were his only national leaders while the Protestant government was not only a religious but also a national oppressor. Moreover, Irish Catholic strength lay in the masses while English Catholicism was predominantly wealthy and aristocratic. In such circumstances the struggle for full emancipation was marked by dissension—between the Catholics in Ireland and the Catholics in England; among the English bishops, particularly between John Milner and the lay leaders of the

English Catholics. When it was thought necessary to obtain a decision from Rome regarding the much-controverted veto power incorporated in a bill proposed in 1813, the confusion was further confounded. For nearly sixteen years the papacy had been disorganized and its business conducted under the greatest of difficulties. One pope had died in exile, the prisoner of the French Republic; his successor, Pius VII. was forced to quit Rome again after Napoleon's escape from Elba. Even the mediation of Cardinal Consalvi, who was the first cardinal since Reginald Pole to be received at the English Court, failed to placate the Irish who showed plainly that their determination not to admit interference in their religion by the British government was greater than their obedience to the Holy See. Shortly afterwards, however, it was the eloquent Daniel O'Connell who, capitalizing on Irish willingness to sacrifice for the faith, united forces in a revitalized Catholic Association, and was largely responsible for the ultimate victory in the emancipation struggle. O'Connell's victory—for the Act of 1829, perhaps more than any other change of equal importance in history, was the personal victory of this one man—was the pledge in law of the permanency of Catholic progress in England.

Although at last Catholics possessed full rights of citizenship, there was little disposition among the approximately 200,000 English Catholics of 1829 to seek new worlds to conquer, or even to attract attention to themselves. This apparent lethargy persisted until the advent on the English scene in 1835 of Nicholas Patrick Wiseman whose importance in the whole English Catholic revival can scarcely be exaggerated. Returning to England in the summer of 1835 after a prolonged residence in Rome where he was rector of the English College, Wiseman was dismayed to find that English Catholics, although freed of their shackles, had not yet shaken off the numbness and cramp which these had engendered. Nevertheless, he continued to cherish high hopes that the time was ripe for the conversion of England to the old faith, and the restoration of Catholics to their former prestige after

long years of abstention from public affairs. He therefore
followed with sympathy and understanding, step by step, the
progress of the Oxford Movement. The greatest mind among
these Oxford men was that of John Henry Newman whose
pamphlet on the apostolic succession which appeared in the
autumn of 1833 was the first of the long series of *Tracts for
the Times* which crystallized the Oxford Movement. After
Newman, the most prominent figures in the movement were
Dr Edward B. Pusey, Canon of Christ Church and Regius
Professor of Hebrew at Oxford, and a number of younger
men including Frederick W. Faber, William G. Ward, and
Frederick Oakeley. Wiseman, in his public utterances and by
his private correspondence with Newman, Ward, and others
did everything possible to turn the movement Romewards.
When in 1844 Ward published his famous *Ideal of a Christian
Church,* in which he denounced the English Reformation
and called upon Anglicans "to repent in sorrow and bit-
terness of heart" their great sin in deserting the Catholic
Church, he was deprived of his degree by university authorities. The final sentence of condemnation which was passed
upon the Tractarians by the Established Church marked the
beginning of an exodus to the Church of Rome. Among the
converts of 1845, Ward preceded Newman whose reception
took place in October of that year. With Newman and Ward
were Ambrose St John, John Walker, Frederick Oakeley,
John Dalgairns, Richard Stanton, Frederick Bowles, and before the year closed, Frederick Faber. The next years saw a
steady flow of converts, clergymen and others, some of them
Cambridge men, who were received into the Catholic Church.

The importance to English Catholicism of the conversions
of such distinguished figures as Newman, Faber, Oakeley,
and Ward cannot be over-estimated. Of great significance,
too, was the fact that the combined intellectual power and
social influence of these Oxford and Cambridge converts created a challenge to the ascendancy of the hereditary English
Catholic families whose distrust of and hostility to the newcomers soon became apparent. It was, perhaps, inevitable

that there should be friction between the enthusiasm of the converts and the extreme self-restraint of the old Catholics who looked askance at the statues, votive candles, hymn singing, and other outward manifestations of religion introduced by Faber at his Oratory in London. The hereditary Catholics with their instinct for caution were likewise annoyed by the critical attitude of the converts on Catholic education and their brashness in revealing the scandals and weaknesses of the Church in their publications.

But while these English converts added to the intellectual stature of the Church, the phenomenal expansion of the Catholic community in England was to come from quite a different source. The increase in numbers was the result of Irish immigration which formed new centres of population in London, Bristol, Liverpool, and other rapidly growing industrial and shipping areas of England. This influx assumed immense proportions during and after the potato famine which began in 1845 and lasted through the two following years. The result of this vast tide of immigration was to change radically the proportional status of native Catholics. In the first quarter of the nineteenth century English Catholics were in the majority, while in the decades after the famine the predominance was Irish. As Manning wryly expressed it, the chief sacrifice he made in becoming a Catholic in 1851 was that he had "given up working for the people of England to work for the Irish occupation in England". Thereafter, though the promising stream of English converts never completely dried up, it became but a trickle in comparison with the Irish torrent. Moreover the unliturgical character of Irish Catholicism tended to check the liturgical revival associated with the names of Dr Daniel Rock, Augustus Welby Pugin, and Ambrose Lisle Phillipps, and which also had the support of Wiseman, a bishop since 1840.

But however Irish the Church of this period in England might appear, the cultural leadership remained overwhelmingly in the English tradition. The Oxford Movement had given the Church numbers of able preachers and writers, men of high cultural stature and intellectual inheritance as a link with a more aristocratic past. And if generations of living together on the part of this Anglo-Irish amalgam failed to restore the general level of Catholic culture to the high plane of its earlier origins in the families of the English Catholic gentry, other gains were made. Not the least of these was the fact that vast numbers of the English-speaking working classes were saved for the Church, in contrast to the losses sustained in Europe which Pope Pius XI lamented as the Church's principal tragedy in the nineteenth century. If this was at the cost of Catholic distinction in cultural and intellectual accomplishments, it is certainly not difficult to understand.

The long years of suffering the evils consequent upon the lack of normal episcopal government in England were now drawing to a close. During the late 1840's the case for the establishment of a more regular ecclesiastical administration was steadily pushed by the two English bishops, Nicholas Wiseman and William Ullathorne. Success crowned their efforts when Pius IX on Michaelmas Day 1850, shortly after his return from exile in Gaeta, issued the apostolic letter, *Universalis Ecclesiae,* which restored the English hierarchy and erected one metropolitan see and twelve suffragan bishoprics. At a consistory held the following day, Wiseman, in his new rôle as archbishop of Westminster, was made a cardinal. His jubilant pastoral dated "from outside the Flaminian Gate of Rome", which formally announced to his countrymen the long-awaited restoration, was destined to set off the alarm against the so-called "Papal Aggression." The press, the Anglican clergy, and leading statesmen voiced indignant protests, public demonstrations were held in London where effigies of the new cardinal were burned in the streets, and other violent manifestations of the popular feeling led to the hooting and pelting of Catholic priests and attacks upon Catholic property. Gradually the storm subsided, and although British hatred of "Popery" continued through the rest of the nineteenth century to war with British belief in religious toleration, principle finally prevailed over prejudice.

Before passing on to a brief review of Catholicism in the rest of the English-speaking world during this first part of the nineteenth century, we may attempt a summary of the progress already achieved in England. By 1850, the Catholic population was estimated at close to 679,000 as compared with 50,000 in 1780, while the number of priests had risen to approximately 800 in England and Wales. Old Orders and Congregations had been revived, new Congregations created, and the hierarchy restored. If socially and economically the poorer Catholics, and these were the mass of Catholics, were the victims of frightful abuses in newly industrialized England, they at least now enjoyed the rights which the government assured all its citizens and could join their fellow countrymen in working for social justice, educational opportunities, and political representation. For those who had experienced the darkness of the past, 1850 offered the bright prospects of what Newman, in his famous sermon to the reconstituted hierarchy meeting in 1852 for the first provincial synod of Westminster, called "A Second Spring".

SCOTLAND AND WALES

In Scotland and Wales, the long penal night of persecution, of exclusion from government, administration, and military service, and of social ostracism, brought about the inevitable decline in Catholic numbers and prestige. As in England, there were Scottish and Welsh families which from pre-Reformation times held tenaciously to their faith, the former located almost entirely in the Highlands, the latter in a few isolated and marginal strongholds such as Holywell in the north, and the Brecon and Monmouth in the south. Presbyterianism had taken over in Scotland early in the second half of the sixteenth century while Methodism swept Wales in the first part of the eighteenth century. To the adherents of both of these groups the Church of Rome was, in the common terminology of the reformers, "the Scarlet Woman," "the whore of Babylon," etc. Under such circumstances, it was not surprising that Catholics in these two countries were a secret people who had learned to keep as quiet as they could about their faith and to make such compromises as were possible. Nor did their situation improve when their numbers were increased by the Irish immigrants who began arriving in the first years of the nineteenth century and reached flood proportions during and after the famine years.

This second great settlement of Scotland from Ireland bore no resemblance whatever to that of the sixth century when Columba and his monks arrived at Iona and spread the faith to the mainland. Most of the nineteenth-century Irish immigrants were employed in and around Glasgow under the most appalling living and working conditions, surrounded by a native Protestant populace to whom their faith and their willingness to work for lower wages made them anathema. By the time Catholic emancipation was achieved in 1829, Glasgow had about 25,000 Catholics in its congregations. When the dominant Irish element among them made heated claims that their interests were being neglected, Andrew Scott of St Andrews is reputed to have said on one occasion, "If yer nac please't wi' the way I dae for yer guid, whatfor dinna ye tak' a sail tae Rome, and see hoo ye come on at the Vatican, if ye ken whaur that is!" Whatever the justice of the complaints, there is no doubt that the situation of these immigrants, weakened by starvation and embittered by the inhuman treatment accorded them by the government of their own country, was a very unhappy one.

Among the first fruits of emancipation in Scotland was the foundation of St Peter's College, Blairs, to replace the small seminaries of Lismore and Aquhorties, and the opening of an Ursuline convent, the first nuns since the Reformation, in Edinburgh. The next step was to restore the strong diocesan government so needed if the Church in Scotland was to prosper. Preliminary negotiations towards this end were spread

over many years, but finally on March 4th, 1878, Leo XIII
in his *Ex Supremo Apostolatus Apice* restored the hierarchy
to Scotland, establishing two archdioceses (Edinburgh and
St Andrews) with the four suffragan sees of Aberdeen, Ar-
gyll and Isles, Dunkeld, and Galloway; and Glasgow, without suffragans, immediately subject to the Holy See. If the
"second spring" of Catholicism in Scotland was not as remarkable as that in England, the former was not altogether
without its share of eminent converts, among whom are outstanding the names of James Hope-Scott, a close friend of
Newman, the third Marquess of Bute, and later the distinguished mathematician of the University of Edinburgh, Sir
Edmund Whittaker.

With the spread of evangelical Protestantism in Wales,
the national ethos became non-authoritarian and non-hier-
archic, in sharp contrast with that of pre-Reformation times.
This practical extinction of Catholicism was due in large
part to the lack of proper ecclesiastical government, but also
to the loss of patrons. Heroic priests continued to serve the
few remaining Catholics until the mid-nineteenth century
when the years of the famine brought a great influx of Irish
into industrialized South Wales. The economic plight of
most of these immigrants was desperate and the hostility with
which they were received by the Welsh did nothing to amel-
iorate their lot. When in 1840, the number of vicars apostolic for England was increased to eight, Wales was grouped
with Herefordshire in a new vicariate. This was obviously
a temporary arrangement, and with the restoration of the
hierarchy in 1850, Wales was divided between two dioceses
which included adjacent parts of England. Though the
Church's progress has been extremely slow among the Welsh
people, it has not been entirely imperceptible, as we shall see
later.

IRELAND

From the twelfth century on, Ireland furnished a classic
example of the greatest of English blunders and the years

following Catholic emancipation were no exception. After 1829 most of the legal discrimination against Catholics was removed in Ireland and throughout the United Kingdom, but the alien Irish Church and alien landownership still remained as standing grievances to which was soon added the issue of national home rule. From the first the religious issue and the religious struggle had been complicated by the national conflict. During the long years of the penal age, the majority of the Irish people remained true to Rome and the faith became a symbol and bond of Irish nationalism. Despite the abject poverty in which they were bound by a land system and other abuses imposed by an alien government, the Catholic majority were forced to pay tithes for the support of the established Church which was in communion with that of England. Daniel O'Connell, successful leader of the emancipation movement, also led the agitation against the tithes, but it was not until 1869 that the Church of Ireland was disestablished.

In the meantime, famine added to the intense sufferings of the Irish to whom relief shipments were sent from all parts of the world, and especially from the United States. In spite of these efforts, hundreds of thousands died while still other hundreds of thousands emigrated to the United States, Great Britain, and other countries. The population which had been growing rapidly in the early part of the nineteenth century and totalled about 8,000,000 in the 1840's, declined sharply to about 6,500,000 in 1851, and still further later in the century. By 1901 the population was less than half what it had been in 1841, and since the economic level of Catholics was lower than that of Protestants, the percentage of loss was somewhat higher among them than among the latter. We have already seen something of what this Irish emigration meant to the English-speaking Church and will return again to touch on the part it played in the growth and character of Catholicism in the United States and the British dominions. As for the Irish who remained in their native land, the remaining decades of the nineteenth century and the opening years of the twentieth continued to be extremely troubled ones which, while serving to intensify their attachment to Catholicism, tended also to increase their hatred of Protestantism and England.

Under Charles Stewart Parnell and his Irish Nationalist Party, the battle for land reform and home rule was fought in Parliament, while outside, the Fenians and other radical societies advocated open rebellion. Meanwhile serious disorders erupted frequently throughout Ireland when Irish tenants refused rent to their landlords and boycotted or shot the landlord's agent or the incoming tenant. In 1882, the Irish cause was seriously injured by the murder in Phoenix Park, Dublin, of Lord Frederick Cavendish, the Viceroy of Ireland, and Under-Secretary Thomas Henry Burke. Although Gladstone's reform included a new Irish Land Act, the problem of alien landlordism was not finally solved until 1903, while the vexed question of home rule was carried over into the twentieth century, becoming acute soon after 1914.

With the country sunken in poverty and absorbed in political agitation, it is not surprising that the Irish Church of the nineteenth century was ill-prepared to resume the characteristics of ancient Irish Catholicism, much less to meet the new challenges of that revolutionary age. When the faith emerged from three centuries of catacomb existence, there was scarcely time to draw a breath before the Church was buffeted by the many problems of the post-emancipation period. Now that it could perform its worship publicly once more, it seemed unable to recall how it had acted when it was free. Thus it seemed content to remain unimaginatively imitative in its church-building, its sacred art and music. Nor did it show any great interest in Catholic intellectual life. The one striking quality which it did preserve from the great Irish tradition of the ancient past was in the contribution it made to the spread of the faith which, as we have already seen, Irish missionaries and Irish emigrants carried to all parts of the world. If their Catholicism was that of post-emancipated Ireland, the results simply prove how greatly the world benefited even from their deficiencies.

THE UNITED STATES

The very years that saw the beginning of a solution to the Catholic question in England and Ireland marked a turning point also in the fortunes of Catholics in North America. Revolutionary leaders, courting support for the patriot's cause wherever support could be found, could ill afford to fulminate against papists or to encourage the persecution of any religious minority. Since expediency and not principle dictated the change, the old hatred of the Church continued to be too useful a weapon to be entirely dispensed with in either England or America where for generations to come there would be those who would not disdain to use it on occasions of political advantage. Although it was many years before the high-sounding language of the Bill of Rights embodied in the federal Constitution was translated into practice in some of the States where even today New Hampshire's constitution is prefaced by a sectarian Bill of Rights in favour of Protestantism, nevertheless American independence presaged the dawn of a better day for Catholics in the new republic.

When war broke out against England in 1774 the juridical bond between the colonies and the vicar apostolic of the London District, under whose jurisdiction they had been, was to all practical purposes abrogated, thereby relieving the English vicars apostolic of a responsibility which they had exercised only with the greatest reluctance and never exercised more than lightly. For the next ten years the only remnant of authority left to govern ecclesiastical affairs was that of John Lewis, the last Jesuit superior, who made no effort to devise a form of clerical administration to guarantee the future security of the Church in the United States. That was to be the work of John Carroll who in June, 1784, was named "Superior of the Mission in the thirteen United States of

North America," and in 1789 their first Catholic bishop with his seat in Baltimore.

Of the nearly 4,000,000 Americans—white and black—in the settlements from Maine to Georgia and in the wilderness to the west, approximately 35,000 were Catholics. Travelling extensively through the infant republic, Carroll laboured indefatigably to serve his flock, most of whom were poor and humble workers. Only a few Catholic families such as the Carrolls themselves and the Brookes, Taneys, and Brents of Maryland possessed sufficient wealth and breeding to command a measure of local respect. Despite their status as an unpopular minority in a predominantly Protestant nation, Carroll and his coreligionists rejoiced in the distinction that was theirs in being the first such group to enjoy political freedom in the modern English-speaking world. That there were, however, many other goals for them to attain if the infant American Church was to win for itself a standing befitting its independent status, no one understood better than the first bishop of Baltimore. For the training of the laity he founded Georgetown College in 1789 immediately adjacent to what was soon to become the nation's capital, while St Mary's Seminary in Baltimore was established in 1791 for the education of candidates for the priesthood. He was greatly aided in his efforts by refugees from Europe, particularly French clergymen who fled the revolutionary upheavals in their own country after 1790. Before his death in 1815, Carroll had also seen the arrival of Augustinians, Dominicans, Franciscans, Trappists, and Ursulines, as well as the founding of several native Congregations of women religious among whom were Elizabeth Bayley Seton's Sisters of Charity, pioneers in parochial school teaching in the United States. Moreover, Baltimore had been raised to an archdiocese in 1808 and the four new sees of Boston, New York, Philadelphia, and Bardstown made subject to it as the metropolitan.

For the quarter century of John Carroll's rule and for many years thereafter, one of the most harassing problems with which the bishops of the American Church had to deal was the issue of lay trusteeism. While there was nothing intrinsically objectionable to the control of church temporalities by the laity, trouble arose when this led to attempts at the usurpation of strictly spiritual powers such as the episcopal prerogative of appointing and dismissing pastors. In Carroll's time controversies broke out in Charleston, Norfolk, Baltimore, and Philadelphia over whether the choice of the priest lay with the congregation which had purchased the land, built the church, and assured the priest of support, or with the bishop. Carroll and his successors contended that once the priest was constituted by the bishop the head of a congregation, the latter had no lawful power or right to dismiss him, but only the right to complain of his neglect, immorality, or incapacity to the bishop who would then be bound to examine the validity of such complaints. These disputes in which the lay trustees were frequently joined by recalcitrant clerics against episcopal authority were by no means infrequent in the years down to the Civil War. In the end the American hierarchy decided to abandon the trustee system as impracticable and a menace to the progress of the Church.

During the Second Plenary Council of Baltimore in 1866 this whole question of the legal tenure of church property was considered anew and the right of the Church to possess property as an essential means to the attainment of its purpose was strongly emphasized. At the time the civil legislation varied widely from the comparatively satisfactory laws finally enacted in New York and other States which allowed bishops to hold property as corporations sole, to the much less favourable conditions obtaining in such States as Pennsylvania. It was but a matter of time, however, until the way was cleared in all States for the Church to legalize its position in regard to its property holdings and thus to end the system. While the resolution of this conflict undoubtedly strengthened the power of the bishops in a way that insured the spiritual good of the Church in the United States, it was unfortunate that the issue served to confirm many American Protestants in their dislike of what they regarded as the exercise of authoritarian power by the Church.

Nationalist prejudices within the Catholic group itself complicated the disciplinary problems arising from trusteeism. Although the reliance of Carroll and his successors in the metropolitan see of Baltimore upon the services of the French refugee priests was quite acceptable to the older Catholic groups of the Maryland-Pennsylvania tradition, trouble came from the rapidly growing Irish element in the Catholic population. Even before the great famine, the immigrant tide from Ireland brought about 650,000 Irish to America in the 1830's. When that tide reached flood proportions after the failure of the potato crop in 1845 and 1846, the sheer weight of numbers of these immigrants inevitably overshadowed the native Catholics. Had the small aristocratic Anglo-American group of the early years been given the time to consolidate their position and to absorb the flow of immigration, the story of American Catholicism would certainly have developed along quite different lines. When the course of events determined otherwise, the tradition of the Carrolls and Brents was all but eclipsed by the new urban Catholicism of the dominant immigrant group. However, as progress was made in Americanizing the Church's foreign-born members, some of the basic elements of the original distinctive American Catholic tradition were preserved. Despite the contest of nationalities which through the years shifted and changed according to circumstances of time and place, the conviction of John Carroll that while Catholics in spiritual affairs must always be true sons of Rome, in temporal and political concerns they were first and last Americans, has remained the inspiration of the American Church and has dictated its policy down to the present day. Because of the tremendous numbers of its immigrant flock and the friction generated at first between the French and the Irish and later between the Irish and the Germans, the challenge presented to the Church in this regard was prodigious. Nevertheless, the efforts it put forth to Americanize its foreign-born members eventually proved singularly successful, although they served also, as we shall see later, to limit its effectiveness in other areas.

By 1850 the Church in the United States had mushroomed to over 1,600,000 of which about 700,000 was due to immigration, and of these over 500,000 had come from Ireland. Presenting the Republic as well as the Church with its first major crisis in assimilation and acculturation, these newcomers were the special targets of nativist opposition and fury in the 'forties and 'fifties. Thus the energies of Catholic leaders were absorbed not only in the immediate task of preserving the religious faith of these immigrants and of assisting them to adjust to the strange environment, but also in protecting them from the strident attacks of the nativists. Compounded of a dislike of aliens and a fear of "Romanism," the nativist attack not infrequently overflowed into mob violence in which depredations were made against Catholic properties and lives. Successive waves of popular hysteria gripped many sections of the country over domestic issues such as the school question and even foreign developments such as Catholic emancipation in Great Britain and the restoration of the English hierarchy. Anti-Catholicism found political expression in the Know-Nothing movement of the 'fifties which became a factor in national politics and enjoyed considerable success in some states and cities. Although the outbreak of the Civil War temporarily silenced the forces of no-popery, a new wave of bigotry began in 1887 with the founding at Clinton, Iowa, of the American Protective Association and swept the country for the next ten years.

In spite of the difficulties within and the opposition from without, the Church in the United States made steady progress. Stretching from coast to coast, the Catholic body at mid-century numbered nearly two million, with over 1,400 priests serving in six archdioceses, twenty-five dioceses, and four vicariates apostolic. Thus when the thirty-two bishops met at Baltimore in May, 1852, for their first plenary council they faced the task of finding solutions for the problems of a truly nation-wide organization. Eschewing any reference to the growing tension over slavery, the conciliar degrees touched on such problems as parochial schools, uniformity of discipline, and administration of church property. John Carroll's insistence that the Catholic clergy of the United States should hold aloof from politics had served the Church well in his day and was to prove a wise course of action during the crisis of Civil War. With some few exceptions, it has been observed by his successors down to the present day.

CANADA

Like the United States, Canada at the beginning of the nineteenth century afforded considerable freedom for the growth and expansion of Catholicism. There, too, the arrival of émigré priests from revolutionary France augmented the clergy, while immigration, particularly from Ireland, added to the Catholic population. The War of 1812 between Great Britain and the United States made the British government again eager not to alienate the French Canadians, a situation which led to further improvement in the status of their Church. Bishop Joseph-Octave Plessis, leader of the Canadian Church from 1806 until his death in 1825, was not slow to seize an opportunity and secured recognition of his title of "Catholic Bishop of Quebec," as well as an annual stipend from the state. He was accorded a seat in the legislative council and, in 1819, announced his plan for four auxiliary dioceses subject to Quebec which, however, was not sanctioned by the government until 1844.

Pioneer work was done in Upper Canada by the Irish priest, Edmund Burke, who later was appointed vicar apostolic of Nova Scotia when it was made an independent vicariate. Thereafter, the major rôle in organizing and enlarging the Church in Upper Canada was assumed by a Highland Scot, Alexander MacDonell, who was named vicar apostolic in 1816, and bishop in 1826. It was the Province of

Quebec, however, with its overwhelming French majority which continued to constitute the main strength of Catholicism in Canada. There new parishes were created and colonization congresses and societies organized, while the Catholic clergy were accorded distinctive privileges and functions such as the right to tithes and the custody of official registers of births, marriages, and deaths which outside the province were kept by civil officials. Closely integrated, thus, with the life of the province, the Church was left undisturbed in its control of its people.

The settlement of Canada's West was, as in the United States, a chapter in which Catholic missionaries played an important part. In the vast area west of Ontario, Catholics multiplied and by 1843 constituted more than half of the Red River Settlement, near the later Winnipeg. The Diocese of St Boniface, Manitoba, created in 1847, was first administered by Joseph Norbert Provencher who invited the Oblates of Mary Immaculate, a congregation of nineteenth-century French origin, to help him. Under the leadership of Alexander Antonin Taché, an Oblate who succeeded Provencher as bishop and in 1871 became archbishop, the Church in the region between Ontario and the west coast made steady progress. Zealous efforts were made on behalf of the Indians and Eskimos with the Jesuits staffing the missions along the northern shores of Lakes Huron and Superior, while the Oblates of Mary Immaculate assumed major responsibility for the Indians farther west.

The problem presented by the Irish emigrants to Canada was even more difficult than that of the nationalities conflict in the United States. Their intense Irish nationalism caused conflict with French Canadians in Nova Scotia and elsewhere. The latter held to their language and customs while the Irish were English-speaking and had their own traditions, stubbornly refusing to be assimilated with the French. Unlike the United States, where second- and third-generation immigrants quickly adopted the English language and tended to conform to the surrounding culture, the prob-

lem of welding together the descendants of French Canadians with those of later arrivals has remained to our own
day.

AUSTRALIA AND NEW ZEALAND

By mid-nineteenth century, Australia and New Zealand
as lands which were peopled almost entirely from the British
Isles displayed, as was to be expected, a predominantly Protestant cast. Anglicans, Presbyterians, and Methodists, with
Baptists and Congregationalists relatively less numerous, far
outnumbered the Catholics. The latter were overwhelmingly Irish, thousands of whom came to escape the frightful
sufferings of the famine years. With the arrival in 1833 of
William Bernard Ullathorne as the first vicar general for
New South Wales, better days were in store for the Australian Church. He and John Bede Polding, who was made the
first resident vicar apostolic for Australia in 1834, were
openly critical of the convict system as well as staunch defenders of religious equality. By 1840 the Catholic achievement was truly remarkable: the number of churches had
increased from one to twenty-five, there were sufficient
priests to serve the existing parishes, a convent of the Sisters
of Charity, a seminary for the training of priests and the
higher education of Catholic youth, thirty-one primary
schools, and a well-organized Catholic population of 23,130.
Among the vigorous Catholic body, Caroline Jones Chisholm
was outstanding for her remarkable work for immigrants and
family colonization. In 1842 a plan of church organization
developed by Ullathorne and Polding was approved by
Rome, eight years before the restoration of the hierarchy in
England. Polding was made archbishop of Sydney, to which
were attached two suffragans, one located at Hobart Town in
Van Diemen's Land, Tasmania, and the other at Adelaide in
South Australia.

In New Zealand, the first vicar apostolic was named in
1842. Six years later the two dioceses of Auckland and Wel-

lington were created, and in 1869 that of Dunedin. Not until 1885 was a regular hierarchy set up with Wellington as the metropolitan see.

SOUTH AFRICA

The Catholic community of South Africa was roughly estimated at 700 in 1837 when the Irish Dominican, Raymond Griffith, was named as its first vicar apostolic. Nine years later, the Eastern Province of the Cape was made an independent vicariate, while four others were established in South Africa by 1892. Race relations complicated the challenge faced by the Church in a land which included a large majority of Africans—Bushmen, Hottentots, and Bantus of various tribes—a large minority of whites divided into Afrikanders and those of British birth or descent, and smaller minorities of Coloured, Indians, and Chinese. In the 1830's and '40's many of the Afrikanders or Boers founded republics to the north—the Orange Free State, the Transvaal, and Natal, to escape British rule. By the end of the Anglo-Boer War of 1899-1902, the three republics had been reduced to submission and in 1910 the Union of South Africa was formally established as a self-governing dominion in the British Empire. Although only the foundations of Catholicism were laid in South Africa in the nineteenth century, a number of Orders and Congregations participated in the effort among whom the work of the Oblates of Mary Immaculate was particularly outstanding. Despite the progress made, the challenge of South Africa was by no means fully met and race tensions remained to become, as we shall see, even more acute in the next century.

TRENDS AND PROGRESS OF THE PERIOD

By mid-century a new era had opened for English-speaking Catholics, but in a world that was becoming progressively less Christian. The gulf that separated the Church from the new liberal order—political, social, and intellectual—of nineteenth-century Europe was profound. The advent of the secular State, frequently conceived in revolution, the problems presented by the advance of science and historical scholarship, the rapid industrialization and urbanization of masses of the people and the resultant flux in social relationships, all taxed the ingenuity of the Church to fit the new circumstances into the traditional patterns of Catholicism. Beleaguered by the bitter hostility of this profoundly secularist world, a certain section among Catholics began to call for a strengthening of the authoritarian element in the Church and vigorously supported the movement for increased centralization of the Church under a papacy of unlimited power. Among the most outspoken of this group was William George Ward who went so far as to declare that he would welcome a definition of dogma every morning with his *Times* at breakfast. It was supporters of this ultramontane persuasion who were intent upon getting a definition of papal infallibility when the Vatican Council was assembled in 1869. They were opposed by extremists of equally questionable zeal such as Ignaz Döllinger in Germany and Lord Acton of England, while moderates like Newman and Félix Dupanloup, bishop of Orléans, argued the inopportuneness of a definition of papal infallibility fearing that it would prove a further and unnecessary obstacle to the wise rapprochement they felt was needed between the Church and the modern era.

When the Council met, Bishop Ullathorne was relieved to discover how moderate were the majority of bishops. Manning led the Infallibilists and threw all his considerable gifts of diplomacy into getting the matter on to the agenda of the Council and securing a definition when it was finally included. But the definition as finally passed was more moderate in tone than some of its proponents had desired and men like Newman and Clifford (bishop of Clifton) who had urged the inopportuneness of the definition before the Council now had no difficulty in accepting it. Save for a few extremists among the English-speaking bishops there was no great enthusiasm for the doctrine and some of the English and American bishops rather than vote against it formed part of the minority of fifty-five prelates who left Rome before the final voting. Thus at the final session only two votes were cast against the definition, one of them being that of Bishop Fitzgerald of Little Rock in the United States. But the minority who had left the Council, as well as Bishop Fitzgerald, accepted the doctrine as soon as it was passed.

With the definition of papal infallibility, the authoritarian and centralizing drives in the Church reached their apogee. While those who had opposed these tendencies were disappointed, there were no episcopal defections such as marked earlier Councils, and the vast majority of Catholic liberals loyally accepted the decisions of the Council. It is not surprising, however, that the conciliar decrees which were products of the pressing needs of the time and represented primarily a defensive, rearguard action against the overpowering assaults of the spirit of the age, led to further misunderstanding of the Church on the part of liberal Europe. Although the result was to stir up rather bitter debate in the English-speaking world where the Catholic body was further severed from the stream of national life, it did not provoke anything like the crippling legislation experienced by the Catholics of Germany and France in the years of the *Kulturkampf* and the Third Republic. Moreover, within the Catholic body of the English-speaking world there remained those, small in number, who refused to abandon their conviction that the best course for the Church lay not in hurling anathemas against the age, but rather in assisting and cooperating with its better tendencies while making no compromise on essentials.

The advent of Leo XIII, who succeeded Pius IX in 1878, gave great encouragement to this group, and his action in bestowing the cardinal's hat on Newman was a symbol of the faint beginnings of that spirit of renewal in the Church, the dramatic fruits of which we are witnessing today. Their long-delayed appearance is accounted for in part by the

Modernist crisis which troubled the peace of the Church just after the turn of the century, and in England resulted in the defection of the convert Jesuit George Tyrrell. While the condemnation of Modernism was necessary if Catholic doctrine was not to dissolve into purely subjective experience, it generated such widespread suspicion and distrust that frequently innocent people became the object of heresy-hunts with the result that Catholic intellectual movements suffered further retardation.

If, generally speaking, the impact on national life and culture of the revived Catholicism of English-speaking countries was inconsequential, and its intellectual resources inadequate to meet the new developments in science and thought of the time, the story of its accomplishments on the practical level affords a much happier picture. Subsequent chapters will treat of the progress made in the development of Catholic educational and other institutions and the growth of a Catholic press, achievements for the most part of a poor, urban, working-class population, many of whom were Irish by birth or by descent. Although the reported increases in the Catholic population of each of the countries of interest in this study need interpretation, there can be no doubt that the century following emancipation saw a numerical growth that was impressive, and in some cases phenomenal. In the United States alone, the Church increased from about 1,600,000 in 1850 to over 12,000,000 in 1900, with the best estimate for 1940 placed at close to 30,000,000. It has since become the third largest body of Catholics in the world, exceeded only by those of Brazil and Italy. Moreover, the figure of 44,000,000 last reported (1963) may be considerably higher if previous studies, indicating that actual figures are usually far above those reported, are valid. The total Catholic population of England and Wales rose from an estimated 679,000 in 1851 to about 3,000,000 in 1950, and stands today (1963) at over 3,500,000. Catholic growth in Scotland was also marked, increasing from about 500,000 in the first years of the twentieth century to the present (1963) figure of nearly 772,000, or about fifteen per cent of the population. Increases in the number of Catholics in Canada, Australia, South Africa, and New Zealand have brought their present (1963) percentages of the total population up to roughly 44 percent, 19 percent, 5.7 percent, and 12.9 percent respectively. In Ireland, emigration has steadily diminished the population so that the number of Catholics in Eire today (1963) stands at about 2,675,000, or 94 percent of the population, while that of Northern Ireland is over 488,000, or about 34 percent of its population. If it is remembered that this century was marked by a general and rapid decline in religious belief and practice, the record of these numerous English-speaking Catholics in maintaining a high level of religious practice becomes all the more remarkable.

After a hundred years of steady growth, the minority status of the Church in the English-speaking world, except for Ireland, remained unchanged. Its predominantly urban cast was also an outstanding feature, for it was not until the middle of the twentieth century that the movement began which took numbers of English and American Catholics out of the heart of urban areas and into the suburbs. The diversity in ethnic origins varied from country to country with the Catholic body in the United States exhibiting the greatest variety of racial and national strains. While the Irish element was strong in all these countries, they also had numbers of Germans as well as southern and eastern Europeans. The appearance of various Eastern Rite Catholics with their own liturgies brought about the establishment in the United States and Canada of separate episcopal jurisdictions with, in some cases, a married clergy.

A radical change ensued for the Church in the United States when a series of restrictive immigration laws were passed in 1921 which gradually closed off the greatest source of increase for American Catholics. The new migration trends following World War II brought an increasing number of Italians, Germans, Poles, and eastern Europeans to Australia thereby strengthening the Catholic Church without, however, upsetting the overwhelming majority enjoyed by immigrants from the British Isles or their descendants. Even Ireland, so long an under-peopled country because of the steady, unremitting emigration which has marked its history since the early part of the nineteenth century, has begun to attract immigrants. By stages, complete independence from Great Britain was finally achieved in 1948, although the connection between Northern Ireland and the United Kingdom which was continued created a problem against which until very recently extreme nationalists persisted in agitating. Already a good many Western Germans, unable to look eastward, have seen the opportunities offered in Ireland and have begun to fill the vacant spaces there.

The vitality of the Church was further evidenced in its efforts on behalf of the aborigines of North America, Australia, New Zealand, and South Africa which over the years were marked by a heroism and devotion deserving of better success than was achieved. While about two-fifths of the American Indians were said to be Christian in 1914, only about half of these were Catholic. In Australia and New Zealand, progress in converting the aborigines to Catholicism was slow, although missionary efforts continued to be expended on their behalf. The inflammable situation caused by unhealthy racial and economic conditions in South Africa created tensions between and within the Christian churches. Catholic authorities denounced the *apartheid* policy as far as segregated worship and unequal employment were involved and, in 1960, they ordained three African priests. Despite retaliatory measures such as the withdrawal of government subsidies to mission schools, the Church continued to pour more and more personnel and funds into South Africa. But with all their growth, the Catholic body in South Africa remained a small minority being only about 5.7 per cent of the total population.

Brief mention should also be made here of the Church's efforts on behalf of the Negro in the United States. Little more than the most elementary religious instruction for Negroes was attempted in the years before the Civil War and that only in a few places. After the war it was, as a leading historian of American Catholicism, John Tracy Ellis, has pointed out, "through a combination of racial prejudice, timidity, and scarcity of manpower and resources [that] the chance for large-scale conversion of the Negroes to Catholicism . . . gradually slipped away." Thus out of a total Negro population today of approximately 19,000,000 only 703,443 are Catholics.

Further evidence of the growth of the Church in English-speaking lands was vividly demonstrated by the rapid expansion of its hierarchical structure, particularly in England, the United States, Canada, and Australia. By 1963, the number of regular episcopal jurisdictions in the United States had increased to 148, in Canada to fifty-nine, England and Wales to nineteen, and Australia to twenty-five. Of the remaining countries, Ireland had twenty-seven; South Africa had twenty; while Scotland and New Zealand had eight and four respectively. Heading these archdioceses and dioceses during this era of growth, were a number of able leaders including the three cardinals who were pioneers of social reform: Henry Edward Manning in England, James Gibbons in the United States, and Patrick Moran in Australia. Other notable members of the English hierarchy included Bishop Ullathorne, Cardinals Wiseman, Vaughan, Bourne, and Hinsley. Among the American prelates who with Gibbons exerted considerable influence on the Church in the United States were John Ireland, John Joseph Keane, and John Lancaster Spalding, to mention only three. While these Catholic leaders, with some few exceptions, failed to grasp fully the intellectual problems which the secular culture posed for Catholic theology, they nevertheless worked actively not only to strengthen the Church but to realize good relations between it and the culture.

This expansion of Catholicism, while in itself no gauge of the essential progress of the Church, had a marked impact on all phases of Catholic life in these countries. The Holy

See, consequently, felt justified in taking action in 1908 to
free the Church in the United States, Canada, England, and
Ireland from the jurisdiction of the Congregation de Propaganda Fide, thus ending their status as missionary territories.
Henceforth, ecclesiastical affairs in these countries would
come under the common law of the Church and enjoy a basis
of equality with the older Churches of Italy, France, and Germany. Among other signs of the maturity achieved in these
years was the increased participation in the Church's far-
flung mission effort which had traditionally been such a striking characteristic of Irish Catholicism but which was now
shared in to a much greater extent by American, Canadian,
English, and Australian Catholics. The marked growth in
the United States of contemplative orders was still another
sign of spiritual adulthood which surprised even American
Catholics themselves but which was part of a world-wide
monastic revival, Protestant as well as Catholic. Still other
pulses of life were evident in the rather tardy spread of the
liturgical movement and the multiplication of various forms
of Catholic Action which made for a more enlightened practice of their faith by the Catholics of the English-speaking
world.

CHAPTER III

INSTITUTIONAL GROWTH

Any understanding of the problem of religion and education as it exists in the second half of this twentieth century demands some grasp of its deep historical roots. Down to the Reformation so traditional was the view that education was a function of the Church that, by the opening of the sixteenth century, education in England had been ecclesiastically controlled for a period of more than 900 years. Schools sponsored by practically every type of ecclesiastical and semi-ecclesiastical institution—monastic, cathedral, collegiate, guild, and chantry schools—were not only all Church controlled but also strongly religious in character. Even the religious upheaval of the sixteenth century did not change the tradition, for the reformers still regarded teaching as wholly a matter for ecclesiastical control, and the Tudors were glad to turn the problem of education over to the Established Church. Some modification was introduced under Elizabeth I when education came to be regarded as subject not only to ecclesiastical law but also to the common law. Nevertheless, the tradition of ecclesiastical control persisted throughout the seventeenth and eighteenth centuries, during which the avowed purpose of schools continued to be religious.

ENGLAND AND WALES

But while there was agreement that schools existed to form Christians, the disagreement on what being a Christian meant resulted in a policy designed to make it virtually impossible to get a Catholic education in post-Reformation England. During penal times, therefore, schools, colleges and seminaries were founded on the continent of Europe to provide the sons and daughters of the Catholic nobility and gentry with an illegal education at considerable risk to all concerned. In spite of the difficulties and dangers, Catholic parents in Britain and even those in the distant American colonies who could find the means, continued to send their children across the sea for the education which the penal laws denied them at home. When the French Revolution destroyed these continental schools and seminaries, they were replaced in the course of years by establishments on English soil. But the task of restoring anything like a complete system of Catholic education was compounded by the revolutionary changes in nineteenth-century thought regarding the relation between education and religion. No longer was there general acceptance of the fact that the two were closely identified in purpose and content, and so the problem of defining their proper relationship was among the thorniest of the century.

Supporters of eighteenth-century Enlightenment questioned the tradition of the past which had left education under Church auspices and argued that the State should administer its own school system, leaving the Churches to find their own agencies for the work of winning each rising generation to their creeds. Moreover, the steady advance of the Industrial Revolution, with its concentration of population in cities, accentuated the controversy over the respective rôles of Church and State in education. The British nation early faced the social problems arising from the birth of a proletariat, and initial leadership for popular education came from religious authorities alarmed by the spiritual apathy of the new factory towns. The task became one of finding an educational blueprint which would satisfy the diverse claims of Catholic parents, Anglican clerics, sectarian fundamentalists, and aggressive secularists. The classic struggle of these forces in the democratic, pluralist societies of the English-speaking world is a complex story which can only be touched upon here in panoramic fashion. Yet some knowledge of it is indispensable for an understanding of the problem which continues to perplex our post-modern era.

The State entered the field of education for the first time in England in 1833 when subsidies were voted to Anglican, and later extended to Catholic and Wesleyan schools. Though financed to some extent by the State, all schools remained under the control of the Churches, but the relative slowness of the latter in providing sufficient places to make compulsory attendance possible, led to further State action. In 1870 a measure was adopted which brought into existence board (or State) schools which would coexist with voluntary (Church) schools. In the course of the lengthy agitation preceding the passing of this bill, sharp differences appeared between the Anglicans and Nonconformists over the question of what religious instruction was to be included in the daily timetable of the board schools. The latter, who held that there should be no mention of religion at all in these schools and that the education which they gave should be wholly secular, finally lost to the Church of England leaders whose solution was incorporated into the Cowper-Temple Amendment. This provided for a daily religious hour of Bible instruction during which, however, no doctrine distinctive of any religious body was to be taught. Moreover, the hour was fixed before or after the periods devoted to the lay subjects so as to permit the withdrawal of children whose parents wished them to sit apart for reasons of conscience.

While the Act of 1870 brought about universal education in England for the first time, the kind of religious formation it inaugurated was destined to work havoc in the religious life of the country. The mass of people educated in the State schools gradually witnessed to the truth of the fact that the lack of definite religious teaching is inevitably associated with an acknowledged lack of any religious faith, and a widespread collapse of elementary morals. Even without benefit of State assistance, Church schools continued to grow, increasing in number from 8,798 in 1870 to 14,275 in 1902, and in the latter year enrolling some 3,729,261 students as compared with the 2,881,155 accommodated in State-supported schools. At the same time dissatisfaction with the educational system grew; agnostics complained about the Bible reading in the State schools, Anglicans and Catholics were unhappy about the heavy financial burden on their schools, and Nonconformists, while satisfied with the Cowper-Temple arrangement in the State schools, complained that in many localities, notably in rural districts, only an Anglican school was available. By the turn of the century, a movement to obtain State funds for the voluntary schools, spearheaded by the Anglicans and joined by Catholics and some few other groups, had gained sufficient strength to force Parliament to take up the question.

After long debate in both the Commons and the House of Lords, the Balfour Bill received royal approval on December 18th, 1902. It provided that the voluntary schools be incorporated into the tax-supported system in order that the efficiency of all Church schools be improved. Endorsed by the Anglican hierarchy, by Cardinal Vaughan, and by many powerful members of the Conservative Party, the bill was bitterly opposed by the Nonconformists and secularists who during the first three years of its operation sponsored a programme of passive resistance which led to the imprisonment of hundreds for non-payment of school taxes. From 1906, when the Liberals swept the Conservative Party out of power, until the beginning of World War I, several unsuccessful attempts were made by the government to repeal the substance of the Education Act of 1902, but a combination of Anglican, Catholic and Conservative forces combined to prevent any change in the basic patterns of this Act.

After the first World War the debate about the place of religion in education continued. Catholic leaders urged their people not to send their children to the State schools where, according to Father Bernard Vaughan, S.J., England's famous preacher, the instruction was "boneless, fibreless, structureless, colourless, tasteless religion, absolutely wanting in every constituent needed to build up the Christian character." Nor were the secularists any better satisfied, arguing that neither the nonsectarian Christianity of the State schools nor the denominational training of the voluntary schools was necessary or desirable for training in character or citizenship. Meanwhile the de-Christianization of England proceeded apace with the number of persons attending church on Sunday reaching alarmingly low figures. In 1944 the Anglicans and Nonconformists sponsored the adoption of a compromise syllabus for the religion courses which was made mandatory for all State schools by the Education Act of 1944. Since the aim of the Act was to complete a coherent national system of primary, secondary, and further education, the religious question was inevitably extended to secondary education. The dividing line was henceforth to be one merely of age, through the transfer of all children at eleven to varying kinds of secondary education (grammar, modern, technical), all equal in status.

Certain features of the Act which received royal assent on August 3rd, 1944, were vigorously opposed by Catholic groups but to no avail. It enjoined on all council schools the daily act of worship and the agreed Syllabus, and it offered certain options to the denominational schools. They could become "aided" by paying half costs; "controlled" by failing to, thereby losing their denominational character except for two periods a week; or "special agreement" schools under an earlier Act. As was expected, more than half of the Anglican schools opted for "control," leaving few except the Catholics to adhere to the old belief in the unity of religious and secular education, or to try to prevent the changed trend from running its logical course. Though the fifty per cent for replacement and expansion costs was more recently increased to seventy-five per cent, Catholics in England and Wales still face a herculean task in keeping their schools in existence in view of constantly rising costs. Thus far, unremitting effort on the part of Catholic bishops and heavy financial sacrifices by their people have maintained a system of primary education designed to keep children out of religiously neutral schools.

In the case of Catholic secondary education, the history for the most part is the story of the different religious Orders, although in recent times the increased participation of the laity in this effort has been a highly significant development. Despite many serious defects arising largely from insufficient resources and lack of coordination, a number of these upper-class schools enjoyed a certain standing especially the Benedictine institutions, Downside and Ampleforth, the Jesuits Stonyhurst, Mount St Mary's, and Beaumont covering the north, middle and south of England respectively, and the school founded by Newman at the Birmingham Oratory which today continues at Woodcote, near Reading, under lay government. An impressive number of convent schools and private academies conducted by the daughters of Mary Ward, the Canonesses of St Augustine, the Dominicans, Benedictines, Franciscans, and even Poor Clares were scattered through the country and enjoyed a long tradition and experience in the education of girls. In addition, many other Orders arrived in England during the nineteenth century including the Sisters of Mercy, the Religious of the Sacred Heart, and the Ursulines, not to mention Cornelia Connelly's Sisters of the Holy Child and other foundations of English origin, adding their influence to the general educational effort.

But during the second half of the nineteenth century, the need to provide secondary education for the Catholic middle class became the great problem. The opening of a boarding and day school at Clapham in 1855 by the Brothers of the Christian Schools marked the beginning of an extensive development which would provide a type of education which was non-classical with a scale of fees suited to the pockets of middle-class parents. This activity in Catholic education continued through the twentieth century but the 1944 Act which raised the school leaving age to fifteen and offered free secondary education of some kind to all has had serious consequences. Most of the existing Catholic schools were of the grammar type, and even these were insufficient. Moreover, if the Catholic system was to keep pace with the national system, Catholic secondary schools of the "modern" or "technical" types were needed into which pupils leaving the primary schools could be graded. Despite the efforts since made to meet these challenges, results still fall far short of the requirements.

To supply teachers for this developing system of schools, existing training colleges were expanded and new ones planned. In May 1963 the English hierarchy announced a plan for the establishment within the next few years of five new Catholic colleges for the training of teachers, the result of long negotiations between the Ministry of Education and the Catholic Education Council. Christ's College, Woolton, Liverpool, is expected to open in 1964 as a co-educational institution conducted by secular clergy and Ursuline nuns of the Roman Union, supported by lay staff. At Leeds, two colleges will be established on the same site, one for men, All Saints' College, the first such institution to be conducted by a completely lay staff, and Trinity College for women under the Sisters of the Cross and Passion supported by a lay staff. The remaining two colleges planned will both be for women students: Cornelia Connelly College at Birmingham and Loreto College at Nottingham, to be conducted by the Society of the Holy Child Jesus and the Loreto Sisters respectively. These four colleges expect to open in 1966.

While nineteenth-century developments covered England with a network of Catholic elementary schools and a growing number of secondary schools, a striking contrast appears when we pass from school to university level. Even today, England has no full Catholic university to which English Catholics desirous of teaching and studying at the highest level may go, nor does it seem at all likely to acquire one in the foreseeable future. The university question was one which was hotly debated during the second half of the nineteenth century as the lack of proper university opportunities for Catholics became more acutely felt. The question of whether English Catholics should take advantage of the gradual abolition of religious tests at Oxford and Cambridge, or create a university of their own as an intellectual coping-stone to the achievements of the second spring, was not entirely an educational problem. Many of the English laity felt that if Catholics were to play their legitimate part in English public life, it was essential that they have access to the full cultural and political opportunities afforded only by Oxford and Cambridge. If this larger social aspect of the question was one which Rome ignored or was ignorant of, and which rigorist theologians in England minimized, it understandably loomed large in the thinking of the laity. It played an important part in the various schemes for Catholic attendance at Oxford which won the support of some of the eminent converts, including Frederick Oakeley and Peter le Page Renouf, but which were strongly opposed by Manning with whom were allied Ward, Dalgairns and in Rome, Mgr George Talbot.

The fact that the Oxford and Cambridge of mid-century which removed the religious tests at matriculation and graduation were rapidly changing from orthodox Anglican strongholds to centres of scepticism and rationalism led to the abortive attempt of 1854 to found a Catholic university in Dublin which Newman as its first rector hoped would be of high standing capable of serving English and Irish Catholics alike. Whether or not it was unrealistic to conceive of Dublin as an intellectual magnet for Englishmen, the only permanent fruit of the venture was Newman's immortal work on the *Idea of a University* which added a classic to English literature. While he continued to concern himself with the problem of how to provide a university education for young English Catholics, Newman's later proposals to return to Oxford to open a college for Catholic students or failing this, an Oratory, were discountenanced by Manning. In 1867 Rome issued an admonition amounting in effect to a prohibition against Catholic attendance at Oxford and Cambridge as a proximate occasion of sin. All things considered, this Roman rescript was regrettable if for no other reason than that it meant the loss of a Catholic Newman at Oxford.

Having effectively crushed Newman's Oxford projects, Manning opened in 1874 the ill-fated Catholic University College in Kensington which from the beginning had little or no prospect of success and was closed down in 1882, having cost the cardinal £10,000. Meanwhile opinion hardened against the Roman prohibition while the number of individual exemptions obtained from the bishops increased in number, without the mass defections from the faith predicted by the Cassandras. It was not until after Manning's death that in 1895 permission for Catholics to go to Oxford and Cambridge under certain conditions was granted. Then it was the clergy who took more immediate advantage of the new opportunities while the numbers of laymen at Oxford and Cambridge did not show any spectacular increase until after 1918 when a tradition of university-going slowly emerged in the larger Catholic public schools. Soon after the edict of toleration, the Jesuits and the Benedictines of Ampleforth opened houses of study for their own subjects at Oxford. These two foundations, now Campion Hall and St Benet's Hall, have become recognized halls of residence and there have been few years when the Oxford class lists have not contained Jesuit scholastics and Benedictines in the first class of Greats and other honours courses. At Cambridge, St Edmund's House was founded for the secular clergy in 1896, the same year that Downside established Benet House, the earliest members of which set a tradition of Catholic scholarship universally recognized as of the highest level. Other Orders followed the example of the Jesuits and Benedictines with the Capuchins and Salesians at Oxford, and the Friars Minor, the Christian Brothers of la Salle, the Irish Christian Brothers, and the Rosminian Fathers at Cambridge adding to the clerical houses established for university study. Dominican priories were opened in both university cities, while Orders and Congregations without houses of their own availed themselves of the facilities offered by Campion Hall and St Benet's Hall at Oxford, and by St Edmund's House at Cambridge.

By the middle of the twentieth century, however, Oxford and Cambridge, though still in a category apart, no longer monopolized the English university world. The development of the University of London, up to 1898 exclusively an examining body, into a regular teaching university of growing size and prestige, and the rise of numerous provincial universities throughout England and Wales have attracted men and women, including many Catholics, from all parts of the country thereby modifying somewhat the local character of these newer institutions. The system of university chaplaincies early sanctioned for Oxford and Cambridge has since been extended, with some modifications, to the provincial universities although many of the problems connected with this work have still to be satisfactorily solved. While the aggregate of Catholics at Oxford and Cambridge is still not proportionate to their total numbers, the contact established with the two national universities was an historic event of major importance for English Catholicism. It not only helped to reintegrate English Catholics into the social and intellectual life of their country, but also greatly benefited their own tradition of scholarship. The experience of expert non-Catholic teaching and of free and informal discussion with people of other mentalities and beliefs, tends to contribute to a valuable process of intellectual cross-fertilization and to produce Catholic graduates better equipped to face the modern world, both at a religious and a secular level.

SCOTLAND

The fundamental issue in the Scottish school question was precisely the same as in England, but the settlement reached in 1918, which has, for nearly half a century, been justly administered, is now regarded as the best in the world. As in England, the earliest period of education in Scotland developed under the supervision of the Church. Foundations for a widespread system of education, including free tuition for the poor were laid by the monks under St Ninian, St Columba, and their successors. Later various other religious Orders came from the continent at the invitation of Scottish rulers and established monasteries and opened schools. Constant warfare with England prevented all but a few of Scotland's scholars from attending English universities, most of them going to one or other of the larger universities of Europe. With the Reformation, Catholics were left with no means of education for their children except for a few illicit attempts at dame schools or tutoring in their homes. Scottish colleges were opened at Rome, Paris, Douay, Ratisbon, and Valladolid to which such youths as could be smuggled out of the country were sent. In the late eighteenth and early nineteenth century a growing spirit of toleration made possible the revival of Catholic schools which were badly needed in the industrial centres where large numbers of Irish and Scottish Catholics sought work in the developing factory cities.

Emancipation came in 1829 to a Catholic body greatly impoverished after the long penal age. Faced with the difficult task of building up and maintaining Catholic schools, the Church in Scotland set resolutely to work and by 1872 had sixty-one Catholic elementary schools which qualified for parliamentary grants. The return of the religious Orders made possible the establishment of some secondary schools under their direction as well as a Catholic teacher training college for women. The inadequacies of the existing system, however, led to the passage by the British Parliament in 1872 of an Education (Scotland) Act which incorporated the principle of one national system supported by State funds made up of local and parliamentary grants. Under this law local school boards were set up which in theory could provide any kind of religious instruction they chose, and in practice, since nine-tenths of the population of Scotland in 1872 were Presbyterians, resulted in the provision for Presbyterian religious instruction in the common schools.

Voluntary schools could transfer their direction to the local boards which would then control and maintain such schools and determine what kind of religious instruction should be provided for them. Provision was made for parents who wished to withdraw their children from such instruction without forfeiting any of the advantages of the secular instruction provided during the rest of the day. While nearly all the Presbyterian voluntary schools were either transferred to the national system or closed down and the children sent to the public schools, Catholics and Episcopalians were unwilling to have their children part of a system in which a Presbyterian atmosphere prevailed. The result was that Catholics made great sacrifices to preserve and extend their schools which as part of the educational system of the country continued to receive government grants if they met the same standards and conditions as those required of the public schools in regard to buildings, courses of study, daily programme, and teacher qualifications. The difference was that voluntary schools received no aid from the local rates as the common schools did and the remaining cost of the Catholic schools had to be met by voluntary contributions from Catholics who, at the same time, were obliged by law to contribute to the support of public schools.

The financial burden thus imposed on Catholics became, by 1918, almost intolerable. The Scottish Education Department studied the problem, meeting informally with representatives of the Catholic Church. The new bill, in addition to widening the administrative area and raising the age for compulsory school attendance, proposed to give the voluntary schools the opportunity to transfer to the public national system under certain conditions. Such schools were to provide as much time for religious instruction as had been customary in the past, and teachers of existing staffs were to be taken over. New teachers were to be appointed only after ecclesiastical authorities had been given a chance to accept their religious qualifications. Any reluctance Catholic leaders felt in accepting the government's proposals disappeared when it became known that the Holy See was in favor of accepting the bill. Subsequently some 226 Catholic elementary schools were transferred and the whole cost of building, equipping, maintaining, and staffing Catholic schools has since been borne by the State, with the schools retaining their Catholic character. The terms were extended to Catholic secondary schools and in places where the numbers of Catholic children did not warrant the building of central Catholic secondary schools, bursaries were given to boys and girls to enable them to attend a Catholic school at some distance. In fact, this kind of aid to Catholics and all other religious groups in Scotland enables them to obtain the kind of education they wish up through the university level.

The entirely new and untried system inaugurated with the settlement of 1918 successfully incorporated the principle of full equality of treatment to denominational schools in Scotland. It involved an adjustment between Church and State which did not violate relations among the denominations. Whatever the relevance of the Scottish solution to other modern democratic nations, it seems clear that the Catholics of Scotland have had no reason to regret their original decision regarding the 1918 Act.

IRELAND

In a triumphal visit in 1963 to the land of his forefathers, John Fitzgerald Kennedy, first citizen and leader of the great Republic of the West, asserted that Ireland and education had been synonymous for nearly 2,000 years. Although in this case history as well as the celebrated Kennedy instinct supports this tribute to traditional Irish eagerness for learning and respect for scholars, the record of educational developments in that troubled land reveals the ups-and-downs not only of the Irish nation but of the English occupying state. Even in their paganism, Ireland's people paid honour to the three privileged classes—the druids, the bards, and the brehons—to whom were entrusted whatever means of education were then available. After St Patrick's time great numbers of schools and colleges were established, chiefly under the monks and priests, although there were also many schools conducted by laymen for the study of law, medicine, and general learning. These schools increased and flourished until towards the close of the eighth century when the Danish invasion led to the break up of many of these great centres of learning. Even after the final defeat of the pagan marauders at Clontarf in 1014, the heritage of ignorance was so great that Ireland did not regain its former prestige as the home of learning. Moreover the Anglo-Norman invasion of 1171 was the beginning of long centuries of strife between native and invader during which education was practically limited to those who intended to enter the Church.

The era of the penal laws, which was even more disastrous, saw a systematic attempt to destroy the Church and all education in the old faith. Public agencies for education including the Royal Free Schools, the Erasmus Smith Schools, the Charter Schools, and the Schools of the Kildare Society, were utilized for the avowed purpose of civilizing the Irish by weaning them from popery. Although, beginning in 1783, the penal laws were repealed, public primary schools in Ireland continued to be used to Protestantize rather than to educate. To remedy this situation, hedge schools multiplied and religious Orders including Nano Nagle's Presentation Nuns and Edmund Ignatius Rice's Irish Christian Brothers opened as many schools as their limited resources permitted. Meanwhile the question of education was being widely debated, and in 1831 a system of national schools was inaugurated designed for both Catholics and Protestants with representatives of both groups on the supervising board. Provision was made for common instruction in general subjects while representatives of the several denominations were to provide separate religious instruction.

From the beginning Archbishop McHale of Tuam was a bitter opponent of the system and refused to allow the national schools to be established in his diocese. Rome, however, left it to the individual bishops to decide the question for their own dioceses. For many years this problem of mixed education continued to be the object of much controversy between Catholics and Protestants, but gradually an increasing majority of the children attended schools which in fact if not in name were denominational. To insure Catholic-trained teachers for their schools, Catholics organized and financed their own teacher-training institutions. Today the Constitution of the Republic of Ireland ordains that free primary education shall be provided by the State. Thus free schools for Catholics, Protestants, and Jews are built, staffed, and maintained by the government, and when necessary, free transportation is provided so that children may attend the schools of their choice.

Up to 1878 Catholic secondary schools in Ireland were few in number and there was no provision for State support and no stimulus for the promotion of secondary education of which Catholics could avail themselves. In that year the Intermediate Education Act gave a strong impulse to the development of secondary education. Funds were provided for the promotion of secondary education without the imposition of unfair religious restrictions, with the consequence that Catholic schools and colleges were improved by abler staffs, better books and methods of teaching, and more improved school apparatus. Catholic youth was thus better prepared to compete successfully in the public examinations, the results of which determined the distribution of public money to the participating schools. The number of secondary schools has grown steadily, while still another feature has been the introduction of technical or vocational instruction.

In the late nineteenth century, the language battle which was one of the points of the struggle in education between Great Britain and Ireland entered a new phase with the establishment of the Gaelic League. For over a thousand years after the introduction of Christianity, the Gaelic language and literature continued to be almost the sole means used to transmit Irish thought and expression. Although the use of the Irish language was proscribed by successive English governments, it was not until the nineteenth century that the language of the Irish people gave way before the many economic, social, and political pressures. When the national primary education system was set up in 1831, it is estimated that there were probably more people speaking Irish than ever before, including a million who knew no English whatever. By presuming that the Irish language did not exist, the new system of education, established on a purely English language basis, wrought havoc with the national traditions in language and literature. The league, founded by the Protestant Douglas Hyde with the assistance of Eoin MacNeill, Father Williams, S.J., and a few others, set about to stem this tide and to save the Irish nation from losing its cultural identity. After arousing interest throughout the country in the restoration of the Irish language, it next sought to have the language re-established in the schools, the professions, and the business world. In 1904 approval was obtained for a bilingual syllabus for use during ordinary school hours in Irish-speaking districts, and in 1922 the government ordered that after March 17th the Irish language should be taught or used as a medium for not less than one full hour a day within the ordinary school hours, in every school where there was a competent teacher. Today although the study of Irish is a required subject in the curriculum of all Irish schools, the language is still in grave danger of dying out.

With the advance of time, primary and secondary education were no longer considered adequate preparation for the average person, and Ireland sought a university for higher education. The Protestant one-third of Ireland had the famous Trinity College in Dublin, but Catholic Ireland for conscience sake was practically shut out from there and from the newer Queen's Colleges of Cork, Galway, and Belfast. Maynooth College, established in 1795, was exclusively for the education of youths preparing for the priesthood. The attempt in 1854 to establish a Catholic university with Newman as its first rector was, as we have seen, unsuccessful.

Finally, however, in 1908 the Irish Universities Act became law setting up the National University of Ireland comprising the College in Dublin started by Newman, and the Colleges at Cork and Galway as its three constituent colleges while St Patrick's College, Maynooth, became a "recognized college" of the National University of Ireland. Today many more Catholics attend Trinity College and it is perhaps symptomatic of the changing Protestant-Catholic atmosphere that the faculties of both Trinity College and the National University were present at the ceremony in Dublin in 1963 honouring Mr. Kennedy at which he declared he felt himself to be part of both and if they ever played each other, he would cheer for Trinity and pray for National.

It was a great triumph for the league when public agitation moved the Senate of the newly founded National University to make a knowledge of Irish a requirement for matriculation. Despite such efforts, there are those who believe that Irish as a spoken language is in grave danger of dying out. Whatever the case, Irish writers such as Mairtin o Cadhain, Tomas Bairead, Liam Gogan, and Sean o Riordain, to name just a few, seem to have achieved considerable success in their attempt to found a modern literature on this language.

CANADA

British North America was no exception to the struggle over education which we have just traced in nineteenth century Britain. Before the British North America Act under which the Dominion of Canada was erected in 1867, an Education Act of 1841 had created separate primary and normal schools for Catholics and Protestants. Although the Canadian Constitution of 1867 made the provinces autonomous in the matter of education, it provided certain safeguards for the rights of those separate schools already in existence in some of the provinces. Nevertheless, in 1871 the provincial legislature of New Brunswick abolished separate denominational schools supported by public funds, and in

1890 Manitoba followed suit. Following vigorous protests, a compromise was effected in New Brunswick in 1874. In Manitoba, in a section where the population was mostly Catholic, a tacit understanding finally permitted the teaching of French and religion in the schools. Eventually, all of the provinces provided free compulsory elementary and secondary non-sectarian education, with many of them making some provision for separate schools for minority groups, mostly Catholics.

Quebec maintained two systems, one Protestant and English, the other Catholic and French. In Ontario, schools might be either public or private, although almost all of the private schools were Catholic and about half of them had French as their language. In Newfoundland all the schools were denominational and financed by public funds. Although Nova Scotia, New Brunswick, and Prince Edward Island had no denominational schools as such, Catholics attended certain schools and Protestants others for which the school boards employed teachers of the same faith as the children. Alberta and Saskatchewan permitted separate schools, but British Columbia did not. Some of the provinces, such as Quebec and Ontario, had Catholic secondary schools as well.

Nor was Catholic higher education neglected. Seeking to maintain the best traditions of French learning, Laval University opened in Quebec in 1854, establishing a branch in Montreal in 1876 which later became the University of Montreal. The Irish-Canadian priest, James J. Tompkins, was responsible for the beginnings of the cooperative movement which later developed into the celebrated programme of adult education associated with St Francis Xavier University of Antigonish. Ontario's educational structure was crowned by the University of Ottawa, conducted by the Oblates. In addition, many other institutions bearing the name of college, some of them affiliated with Laval University or the University of Montreal, were founded in the nineteenth and first half of the twentieth century. A further notable achievement was the establishment of the Pontifical

Institute of Medieval Studies in Toronto which while independent of the University of Toronto, had an arrangement whereby its degrees were granted through that institution. The Institute's extensive collection of medieval manuscripts has made it a major centre for research in that field.

The emphasis on French in the Catholic schools of the Dominion was a reflection of the fact that the French constituted numerically about two-thirds of the total Catholic population of Canada. Although the Church also made careful provision for the one-third of the faithful who were not French by descent and language, Catholicism in general tended to be identified with French life and institutions. This accounts in large part not only for the difficulties that arose in regard to schools in the various provinces, but also for the tension in relations between the federal government and a growing French-Canadian nationalist sentiment, of which the 1963 disturbances in Quebec were an expression.

AUSTRALIA AND NEW ZEALAND

As in British North America, the question of State support of church schools became a cause of bitter controversy in Australia and New Zealand also. Initially the general policy was to have all schools conducted by the various denominations and aided by subsidies from the State. However, in 1841 New South Wales provided for the setting up of common schools where no other schools existed, and subsequently two boards were formed, one for the denominational and the other for the common schools, with State aid divided between them. But under the impact of liberal and rationalistic thought, legislation was passed in all the Australian States which established free, compulsory, secular elementary education and which cancelled State aid to denominational schools. With national education taking a turn which Catholics claimed they were not able in conscience to follow, the Church set about creating a complete school structure of its own which, without State aid, depended largely for its existence upon the religious Orders. A growing population and rising costs have obliged Australian Catholics to increase their voluntary contributions while at the same time they must pay increased taxes to support schools they cannot use. Thus through the years the fight for the schools has been unceasing, but the great defeat of the 1870's has never been reversed although a Commonwealth scheme in 1952 provided a concessional deduction in taxable income for education expenses. While the policy itself indicated an important shift of opinion, the amount of the concession was so negligible as to afford scarcely any relief to the Catholics who needed it most.

On the secondary level also, an increasing number of Catholic schools both of the academic type and technical type were opened, though neither kind ever caught up with the problem of catering to the huge numbers concerned. Most of these secondary schools, including the newer parochial or inter-parochial type as well as the older schools, were staffed by the various religious Orders, who in many cases also conducted central training colleges for prospective teachers.

On the university level, the early precedent set in Sydney of a non-denominational university with affiliated denominational colleges became the official mode of university education for Catholics in Australia. Thus St John's, within the University of Sydney, was incorporated in 1857 and opened in 1860. In the following year application was made for a similar Catholic college at the University of Melbourne, but it was not until the second decade of the present century that the proposed institution was erected and dedicated to the memory of John Henry Newman. St Leo's College, within the University of Queensland, was established in 1917, and, in 1949 Aquinas, in the University of Adelaide. Colleges for women followed including Sancta Sophia incorporated in Sydney in 1929 as a sister college to St John's while Duchesne was established later in Brisbane. In the years following World War II the attempt to establish a Catholic university in Sydney was considered by Archbishop Mannix of Melbourne to constitute a grievous error. There were many in Australia who shared His Grace's sentiments in this matter and who viewed with relief the failure of the attempt.

In New Zealand's early years, the legislatures of the provinces into which the colony was divided subsidized denominational schools. When, however, the provincial legislatures gave way to a centralized government in 1875-1876, aid to denominational schools was abolished and a national system of free, secular, and compulsory elementary education was introduced. As in other countries, the Catholics of New Zealand refused to send their children to schools from which religion was excluded and at enormous sacrifice built up a system of parochial schools which were as closely supervised by the government as the State schools. Constituting less than twenty per cent of the total population of New Zealand, Catholic persistence in asking for State aid for their schools met with little or no success.

SOUTH AFRICA

Catholic education in the Union of South Africa had to contend not only with the usual problems of finances and personnel, but also with the more difficult questions of linguistic differences which until quite recently associated the Church almost completely with the English-speaking section of the community, and with racialism in the form of *apartheid,* which was put into effect after the election of 1948. The history of Catholic schools began with the arrival of the first bishop, Raymund Griffith, at Capetown where he founded an academy for boys. Most of the early missionary priests established some sort of school in the areas they served. The latter part of the nineteenth century saw the arrival of the teaching religious Orders in Cape Colony and Natal. Grants-in-aid were made by the government to some of these Catholic schools down to the Anglo-Boer War, after which the British authorities in the Transvaal and Orange

River withdrew support from denominational schools on the ground that the State schools were providing suitable education. After the Union of 1910, education was left to the provinces where partial aid was given to Catholic schools in the Cape Province and Natal, leaving Catholics elsewhere in the Union to assume the full financial burden for separate education.

Unfortunately, the Church's primary missionary effort was confined to the scattered Europeans of whom Catholics were only a very small element. In the task of Bantu education, Catholics began a half century or more after the Protestants, while it is only very recently that the Church has penetrated at all into the world of the Afrikaans-speaking people. The result has been that Catholicism has not been very influential in guiding the course of the almost fanatical growth of Afrikaner nationalism on the one hand, or the spread of militant African nationalism on the other. However in 1951, with the establishment of the hierarchy, the Church has come of age and has launched forth on a more active and direct policy of evangelization. The Bantu Education Act of 1953 providing for the progressive withdrawal of government subsidies upon which mission schools had come to depend, created a crisis of serious proportions, the outcome of which is not yet determined. Catholics declared their intention of assuming the staggering financial burden of keeping their Bantu schools open as far as possible without the subsidies. Nevertheless, by July 1959, approximately sixty schools had closed and the total number of pupils had dropped from 112,000 to 93,000. None of the six Catholic training colleges had been granted the recognition which the Act required, and the qualifications of the teachers trained in them were thus not recognized. Three of these had closed, as well as ten Catholic secondary schools for Africans, including four of the largest in the country. Other laws such as the Group Areas Act of 1950, which aimed at achieving maximum separation between the races, have also been the cause of substantial losses. As the government makes extensive use of the powers conferred upon it in such legislation, it threatens to disrupt completely the Church's educational and other undertakings. There is grave reason for the fear that the day may come when white missionaries may be excluded from non-European areas, and the training by Europeans of non-white aspirants to the priesthood and religious life forbidden.

THE UNITED STATES

In the United States the growth of a completely Catholic educational system from the kindergarten to university and professional schools has been called the greatest single achievement of American Catholicism. It is all the more remarkable when one recalls that during the colonial period the penal laws forbade Catholics to maintain their own schools so that the national period opened without a single Catholic educational institution. Although it was no easy task for the bishops of the United States to provide at once for the religious and the educational needs of their people, the example set by John Carroll who founded Georgetown Academy in 1791 was faithfully followed by his successors. Because nineteenth-century public schools were to all intents and purposes Protestant schools, the Church was impelled in the face of almost insuperable difficulties to establish its own schools, often side by side with the public schools. By the twentieth century, the prevailing ideology of the public schools, at least in the larger urban centres, became secularist rather than Protestant with religion systematically excluded from education. American Catholics, retaining their conviction that no genuine education was possible unless it was religiously grounded and religiously orientated, felt the need for their own schools more insistently than ever. Moreover, since World War II, they have joined the many Protestants and the less numerous Jews who favour retaining in the public schools what little religion is left, on the premise that the acknowledgement of God's existence is part of the national tradition and helps, in a small way, to preserve the public school from a bias against religion. In this they are opposed by the secularists and some Jewish groups who want the last traces of religious activity removed from the public school.

Both the religious school and the various programmes of religion in the public schools have raised the bitterly controversial question of Church and State in education. Catholic demand for state aid for their schools, more or less spasmodic in the past, has currently taken on new intensity. Despite the fact that by 1963 there were some 10,776 parochial or private elementary schools with 4,609,029 pupils, and 2,433 secondary schools enrolling 1,004,927 students, the Church is still not reaching even a majority of its children through its own schools. Moreover, the dimensions of Catholic education in the future are such that its costs will be beyond the ability of the Catholic people to bear unaided. Many argue that sooner or later Catholics will cease to add to their elementary school commitments or will abandon them entirely. On the other hand, others see a striking shift in public opinion on the question of federal aid to private schools. A Gallup Poll in March of 1961 revealed that fifty-seven per cent of those polled held that federal aid should go to public schools only, and thirty-six per cent thought it should also go to private and parochial schools. In February, 1963, the same poll showed that only forty-four per cent would now restrict aid to public schools alone, while forty-nine per cent would want it to go to private and parochial schools as well. Other significant developments include the recent attack of Dr Robert M. Hutchins, President of the Fund for the Republic, on the "wall of separation" metaphor used by many to describe the ideal relationship between Church and State, but which he saw as an obstacle "hampering us in our search for a national idea of education and a national programme to carry it out". The veteran political analyst, Walter Lippmann, also pointed out that parochial schools are part of the American system of education and, in his opinion, it cannot be beyond the wit of man to find a way of aiding them.

On the Catholic side of the debate, the issue is now being argued more calmly and moderately without the indignant official protests, suggesting that Catholics would torpedo any education bill in which their interests were ignored, which marked some previous discussions. New winds are also blowing in both Catholic and Protestant sectors on the parallel problem of religion in the public schools. Recent decisions of the Supreme Court declaring unconstitutional provisions for the optional use of prayer and Bible-reading in public schools dramatized the extremes to which the secularizing tendencies at work in American society have developed. While reactions have varied in both Catholic and Protestant groups, these decisions were not popular with the vast majority of the American people. Disturbed by the alarming increase in juvenile delinquency, many Americans who formerly were indifferent to the question of religious education are now having sober second thoughts. Recent proposals include a plan for "shared time" which allows the child's school time to be shared between neutral public schools and church-supported schools which teach subjects with specifically religious content. Other suggestions from Catholic sources for financing parochial schools from a central school fund, either for a whole diocese or for each of several districts within a diocese are likewise being tried. But a fully satisfactory solution to this problem which has baffled generations of Americans of all religious beliefs has yet to be adopted.

When we turn to the field of higher education, the record of Catholic expansion as the twentieth century progressed was increasingly remarkable. Catholics had founded colleges early in the nation's history, but the period of most rapid growth came after World War I. At present some 267 Catholic colleges and universitites have a combined enrollment of about 322,000 students and are maintained by priests or religious, with the sole exception of a recently incorporated Catholic university in Connecticut under the direction of a group of laymen. For the most part, these institutions adopted the pattern of a four-year course common in the

colleges of Protestant origin. While colleges for women appeared somewhat later than those founded by Protestants,
they eventually outnumbered the Catholic colleges for men.
All too many of these Catholic institutions, however, came
into being with no planning even on a diocesan scale, to say
nothing of the question of national needs. Furthermore, there
was little evidence in many cases that those responsible had
any true comprehension of what this growing commitment
to higher education in itself implied. One of the outstanding
exceptions was John Lancaster Spalding, Bishop of Peoria,
through whose persistence, intelligence, and resourcefulness
The Catholic University of America opened at Washington in
1889. Given the circumstances of the time vis-à-vis the Catholic Church, it was not surprising that the university did not
immediately realize all its founder's hopes of furthering the
intellectual prestige of American Catholicism. What was
astounding and humiliating to American Catholics who are
called upon annually to contribute to the support of this
same university, was the action in the winter of 1963 of its
administration in banning four theologians as possible
speakers in a public lecture series which subsequently became
an international *cause célèbre*.

The university's official explanation of why the names of
Fathers John Courtney Murray, Hans Küng, Godfrey Diek-
mann, and Gustave Weigel were struck from a list of prospective speakers was that the controversial views of the four
might seem to commit the university to one side of several
matters still to come before Vatican Council II. It soon became clear that such timidity on the part of the authorities in
relation to theological and other academic discussion was
not shared by most of the university's faculty.

Marked as was the advance made by Catholic higher education, it has yet to catch up with that begun by Protestants
and supported by them or the State. The failure of Catholics
to make a cultural and intellectual contribution proportionate to their numbers and their consistent emphasis on educa-

tion has confirmed many in their doubts of the expediency and efficiency of American Catholic higher education. It may also account in part for the preference European Catholics have for a public school system and for theological faculties integrated in the great State universities, rather than separate institutions cut off from the centres of intellectual life. The self-criticism of some of the American Church's leading educators has resulted in proposals for better planning and staffing, improved curricula and much-needed consolidation which give grounds for restrained optimism about the future. In addition, a striking reversal in the attitude to religion on the part of leaders in State universities and other major institutions of higher learning has resulted in the employment of Catholic clerics as professors of religion in such institutions as Western Michigan University, and the State universities of Iowa, Kansas, Montana, Missouri, and Tennessee. Even Dr Leo Pfeffer, outspoken opponent of any religious intrusion in public elementary and secondary schools, found no legal objection to such courses in tax-supported colleges. With much of the world's future being moulded on the campuses of secular and non-Catholic colleges and universities, the Church has a mission not only to enter that society to communicate and associate with it but eventually to redeem it. Cooperative programmes provide still another opportunity for fruitful exchange between Catholic and other institutions of higher education and may be greatly expanded in the future if there is any validity in the recent forecast by the Association of American Colleges for higher education in the United States in 2000 A.D. The twenty-five million college and university students of that year will, according to this prediction, pass from a junior college with an A.A. or A.S. degree. Universities will have dropped freshman and sophomore years; graduates from junior colleges will enrol for a three-year programme leading to a master's degree. In the process most liberal arts colleges, including Catholic, will turn into junior colleges.

Impressive as they are, the results of this gigantic Catholic educational effort in the English-speaking world have not escaped close and critical scrutiny in recent years. Even allowing for the inevitable pull of a majority upon a minority, it must also be admitted that the extensive leakage and widespread abandonment of religious practice has been partially caused by a mistaken method of religious instruction. The exaggerated conceptualization of religion and the negative emphasis on obligations and commandments are at present giving way before the catechetical renewal with its kerygmatic approach and existentialist emphasis on personal commitment. Furthermore, a new lay spirituality is slowly emerging to replace the monastic spirituality which in the past was imparted to the majority of English-speaking Catholics by the religious teachers under whom they were trained. While it is true that these religious teachers made possible the separate system of Catholic education which was the Church's uncompromising protest against the liberal and secular tendencies of the nineteenth and twentieth centuries, it may also be true that such a system was no more than a temporary measure hastily designed to meet these crises. Certain it is that there is nothing in the Church's definitions on education that makes such a system essential or even desirable. Moreover, the constant pressure for more and more schools has strained the existing staff almost to the breaking point, while for many decades now the increase in candidates for the teaching Orders has not kept pace with the increase in the Catholic population. Employment of an increasing number of lay teachers appears to be the only means whereby Catholics can preserve their independent system, and in such an eventuality a point may be reached where the structure of the system could change, with education becoming chiefly an area of lay concern as the religious withdraw to other more needed forms of the apostolate.

CHAPTER IV

THE CATHOLIC PRESS

ENGLAND

While Catholic journalism in the English-speaking world dates back to the last years of the eighteenth century, most of the early ventures were short-lived. The real beginnings of a Catholic press in England were made in the post-emancipation years when the growth of the Catholic population with its newly won freedom, the progress of Catholic education, and the Oxford converts with their superior intellectual abilities and religious zeal all combined to emphasize the importance of such a medium. Modest in its beginnings, the English Catholic press sought and, at times, succeeded not only in chronicling events but in influencing them. Of the several attempts of the 1830's and 1840's in England, two Catholic publications were destined to survive and to play an important role in the future history of Church and country: the *Dublin Review,* Wiseman's quarterly founded in 1836, and a weekly newspaper, *The Tablet* of London, founded in 1840 by Frederick Lucas, a convert from Quakerism. In spite of its name the *Dublin* was an organ of English not Irish Catholicism and from the outset was edited and published in London. Its August 1839 issue carried Wiseman's article comparing the position of the Donatists with that of the Anglicans which Newman later confessed exercised a decisive influence on his conversion to the Catholic faith. Subsequent issues carried articles by Newman himself and many of the other converts which ultimately established a reputation for the *Dublin* on both sides of the Atlantic. When

Manning took over the review from Wiseman in 1862 and found in the person of the convert lay theologian, William George Ward, an editor in complete agreement with his extreme authoritarian views, the sympathy of some of the more liberal Catholic thinkers was alienated.

During this period men like Newman in England and Orestes Brownson in the United States saw the need for a Catholic review which could critically evaluate the philosophical, social, and political problems of the day and opposed the attitude of Ward and others who wished every question settled authoritatively from Rome. There can be little doubt but that the *Dublin* became a platform for the expression of Ward's temperament and mentality and that his work served to deepen the general antagonism to the Church in England. However, with the editorship of Wilfrid Ward, which began in 1906 just twenty-eight years after his father's resignation of the same post, the *Dublin* entered its most distinguished period. Free from official inspiration, it put forward a presentation of Catholic opinion at once orthodox and adapted to modern needs, reflecting modern knowledge and using modern language. Following Wilfrid Ward's retirement in 1915, the tradition of the *Dublin* was in varying ways carried on by his successors including Shane Leslie, Algar Thorold, Denis Gwynn, Christopher Dawson, T. S. Gregory, T. F. Burns, and Norman St John-Stevas under whom, in 1961, it became the *Wiseman Review*.

Frederick Lucas, pioneer of the Catholic newspaper and editor of *The Tablet* from 1840 to 1855, was a man of absolute views who found it difficult to speak or write with moderation on most subjects. This fearless and eloquent champion of the Catholic cause frequently dismayed those Catholics who, unaccustomed to a newspaper of their own, were inclined to think discretion the only policy. When *The Times* and Lord John Russell raised the "papal aggression" outcry against the re-establishment of the hierarchy, the militant Lucas did more than any other individual except Newman to hearten the timid Catholics of England and Ireland.

His uncompromising views and political activities inevitably brought him into conflict with the Irish bishops, and he was forced to appeal to Rome in 1854 shortly before his death. His successor, John Edward Wallis, not only brought *The Tablet* back to London from Dublin where Lucas had transferred it, but also initiated the long association with conservative principles for which the paper is still known. In 1868 he sold *The Tablet* to Father (later Cardinal) Herbert Vaughan, and it was not until 1936 that the paper returned to lay control when Cardinal Hinsley sold it to a group of laymen including Douglas Woodruff, the present editor. An Oxford scholar whose previous experience included writing for *The Times,* Woodruff had swift access to important information, and he soon made *The Tablet* a source of news, especially in foreign affairs, not to be found elsewhere.

Quite different in character was the *Rambler,* begun as a weekly journal in 1848 by another convert to Catholicism, John Moore Capes, and destined to develop into one of the most distinguished reviews ever published in England. While a great deal of work of lasting value and importance appeared in the *Rambler* under its successive editors, including Richard Simpson, Newman and Sir John (later Lord) Acton, it was little understood or appreciated by the Catholics of the day most of whom regarded it with increasing distrust. Burning to see the Church take advantage of its emancipation and become, once again, a community on the march, the supporters of the *Rambler* sought an adequate intellectual presentation of Catholicism in nineteenth-century terms. Critical of tradition and disrespectful of ecclesiastical authority, Simpson and Acton, at times, went to such extremes as to alienate even the usually sympathetic Newman. But if it was unfortunate that Acton and his associates were so injudicious in their theological excursions and so determined to be independent of the hierarchy, the really tragic aspect of this period was the official suspicion and distrust which contrived to block even the most sincere attempts to make Catholicism a creative and revivifying force. As articles on the relations of faith and reason, on Tridentine seminaries and their deficiencies, on toleration, on original sin, and on eternal punishment made their appearance in the pages of the *Rambler,* the bishops grew more and more uneasy.

In 1862 the name of the journal was changed to the *Home and Foreign Review* and the intention to abstain as far as possible from theological discussion was announced. The crisis came when the review reported on the Munich congress of 1863 and Professor Johann Döllinger's address there calling for a complete reorientation of the Church's policy, for the abandonment of scholastic philosophy, and for the maximum of speculation and discussion and the minimum of authority. Hailing the address as one of "rare significance", Acton declared it would bear fruit for the whole Catholic world. Among the first fruits it bore was the untimely death of the brilliant English periodical, for when Pius IX sent a condemnatory brief to the archbishop of Munich in December 1863 Acton followed with the announcement of the discontinuance of the *Home and Foreign Review* in April, 1864. The loss not only impoverished English Catholic intellectual life so that it fell more and more below that of the rest of the country and exercised no influence on the public mind; it likewise served to discourage all who by writing or public service of any kind might wish to advance the cause of religion as independent laymen. It is not without contemporary significance that this frustration of the movement in support of a more lively and intelligent role for the laity in the Church tended to perpetuate the concept of the layman as a kind of spiritual "boy eternal" for nearly another hundred years. Fortunately, however, present-day developments are more heartening. Lay initiative is, with papal encouragement, on the increase and there is a growing understanding of that abiding vision of Newman's that the fullness of the Catholic idea demands that the laity should participate more actively in the life of the Church.

Of the numerous other English Catholic publications of various periods, the *Month* founded in 1864 continued down to 1949 as a Jesuit organ of high quality. Then the new editor, Father Philip Caraman, initiated a completely transformed New Series making it a literary review with poetry, fiction, art questions, and belles-lettres generally, as well as specifically religious and philosophical topics. The new venture was hailed as "a striking success" by non-Catholic as well as Catholic critics, including the *Times Literary Supplement* and T. S. Eliot.

In the mid years of the nineteenth century, with the abolition of the tax on newspapers and the duty on imported paper, the first signs of the new age of mass communication appeared when the London daily papers came down to a penny. The first Catholic penny paper with permanent success was the London *Universe,* published initially in 1860. Recent years have seen a contraction of the literary side of the paper with a definite precedence of news over views and the adoption of other methods of ultra-modern journalism which have enormously increased the circulation. The *Catholic Times,* brought out first in 1867 by Fr (later Mgr) James Nugent of Liverpool, the celebrated temperance apostle, was also modernized, but retained more of its original character remaining the favourite newspaper of a great many Catholics of Irish origin or extraction. Modernization, however, was not successful in saving the paper and it was absorbed by the *Universe* in 1962. The *Catholic Herald,* founded in 1884, was completely transformed when in 1934 it was taken over by a group of laymen. Ably edited for nearly twenty years by Count Michael de la Bédoyère, this newspaper proposed to deal with news and events of all kinds from a Catholic standpoint and its efforts met with considerable success.

Only the briefest mention can be made here of such learned publications as the *Downside Review,* founded by Abbot Aidan Gasquet, O.S.B., in 1882, to deal with questions of theology, philosophy and monastic history; *Blackfriars,* the organ of the Dominicans at Oxford, founded in 1920 by Father Bede Jarrett, O.P., to give the Church's view on the problems and questions of the hour in the great tradition of the Order; and lastly of the *Clergy Review,* a monthly founded in 1931 with the object of taking fuller account of the special problems and interests of the clergy than could be expected of any existing periodical.

SCOTLAND

Catholic journalism in Scotland did not begin until late in the second half of the nineteenth century, and to date no Scottish Catholic daily paper has ever been published, although such a project has been considered more than once in Glasgow. It was not until 1885 that the *Glasgow Observer* finally came into existence, and it remains today the only Catholic weekly newspaper published in Scotland, serving the Catholics of the southwest of Scotland, and, as the *Scottish Catholic Herald,* those of the eastern and northern districts of the country. A number of Irish and English Catholic weeklies, such as the *Irish Weekly,* the *Catholic Times,* and the *Universe,* subsequently provided Scottish editions. A monthly, the *Mercat Cross,* begun in 1951 by the Jesuit Fathers of Edinburgh, has met with considerable success. For the most part, Scottish Catholics have been content to use the specialized periodicals published in England or Ireland, but in 1950 the first specialist journal produced in Scotland appeared as the *Innes Review,* an organ of the Scottish Catholic Historical Committee.

IRELAND

Although at first glance the number of Ireland's Catholic papers and periodicals appears strangely limited, the apparent anomaly is explained by the fact that the greater part of the country's general press reflects the fundamental position which the faith occupies in the everyday life of the people. Thus, while there is no distinctly religious daily published in Ireland, such papers as the *Irish Independent, Irish Press,* and *Evening Herald,* printed in Dublin, the *Cork Examiner,* and the Belfast *Irish News* are whole-heartedly Catholic in their presentation of news. Two Catholic weekly papers, the *Irish Catholic,* founded in 1888, and the *Standard,* which has a considerable circulation in Britain, specialize almost exclusively in religious and ecclesiastical news. Most of the remaining weekly newspapers devote a reasonable amount of space to Catholic matters. Although Irish Catholic magazines and quarterlies like *Studies* and the *Irish Ecclesiastical Record* compare favorably with periodicals of similar type in other countries, there is, regrettably, a dearth of first-rate philosophical, theological, historical, and liturgical reviews.

AUSTRALIA, NEW ZEALAND AND SOUTH AFRICA

Catholic journalism in Australia had a long and difficult road to travel before reaching its present position in size, quality, and influence which easily surpasses the rest of the religious press in the country. Beginning with the *Chronicle,* founded by a group of laymen in Sydney in 1839 to answer the attacks on Catholicism in the existing newspapers, the way was marked by many failures. Today, however, the Church has its weekly newspapers in each State of the Commonwealth which continue to reflect that vigorous tradition in defence of freedom and social justice associated with Australia's history. A quarterly, the *Australasian Catholic Record* founded by Cardinal Moran in Sydney in 1894, is of interest mainly to priests.

For the most part, the history of Catholic journalism in New Zealand is the history of the *Tablet,* a weekly founded by Bishop Patrick Moran of Dunedin in 1873. Its early period was associated with the battle for Catholic rights. From the first the paper was fortunate in its editors who made it a respected organ in the land. A fortnightly, *Zealandia,* published at Auckland, likewise circulates in all parts of the country.

In South Africa, too, the Catholic press came into being

to meet attacks on the Catholic religion, and the Grahams-town *Colonist,* the first weekly, founded by Bishop Aidan Devereux in 1850, continued in that tradition for a period of about ten years. In 1891 with the appearance of the *Catholic Magazine,* a monthly edited by the scholar-priest Frederic Kolbe, Catholic effort in journalism and apologetics ceased to be episcopal. Not an official organ, the magazine did not limit its subject-matter to expounding the dogmas of faith but expanded its treatment to cover a wide range of topics on the relation of contemporary thought to Catholic belief. Characterized also by better scholarship, the *Catholic Magazine* circulated over the whole country and won the respect of many who were not Catholics.

CANADA

Canada's French origins are reflected in the history of its Catholic press which can be traced back to *Le Canadien,* the first periodical of importance founded in Quebec in 1806 by Pierre Bédard. The first English Catholic periodical was the *Catholic,* founded in 1830 and edited by Bishop Alexander MacDonell in Kingston and later moved to Hamilton where it was published from 1841-1844. Today English and French Catholic publications flourish throughout the ten provinces of Canada, among which *Action Catholique,* a French daily published in Quebec since 1907, and *Ensign,* English Canada's national news weekly, deserve special mention. The inspiration for the latter sprang from an audience which Robert W. Keyserlingk and Murray Ballantyne had with Pius XII in May, 1946, in which the pope spoke of the duties of the press in writing and reporting truth. From its first issue in 1948, the *Ensign* has expanded its staff and grown into an authoritative organ which is quoted in England and the United States as well as throughout Canada. Magazines in French and English are published by many of the religious Orders of Canada, including the Jesuits, the Redemptorists, the Holy Cross Fathers, and the Oblates of Mary

Immaculate. Noteworthy among the university publications are *Laval Théologique et Philosophique* of Quebec, the *Revue de l'Université d'Ottawa* and *Medieval Studies* of the Pontifical Institute in Toronto.

THE UNITED STATES

The *United States Catholic Miscellany,* established in 1822 by Bishop John England to explain the true doctrines of the Church and to answer the calumnies of its enemies, was the first American Catholic weekly newspaper properly so called. The example of the first Bishop of Charleston was soon imitated by Catholics in other parts of the country so that two decades later there were about twenty weeklies for the English-speaking Catholics, as well as the *Wahrheits-freund* of Cincinnati, initially published in 1837 as the first of a long series of German Catholic newspapers in the United States. Responding to the nativist attacks with vigour, these newspapers were also an important means of instructing the growing number of Catholic immigrants in their faith and the ways of American life. While many of these pioneer efforts of the first half of the nineteenth century were not conspicuously successful according to present day standards, the accomplishments of James A. McMaster and Maurice Francis Egan of the *Freeman's Journal* in New York, and Thomas D'Arcy McGee and John Boyle O'Reilly of the *Pilot* in Boston, to mention just a few, helped to make journalistic history.

Perhaps the most outstanding critic and journalist of the time was the convert Orestes A. Brownson whose career as a stormy and implacable controversialist was not unlike that of Frederick Lucas of the London *Tablet*. In the *Review* he founded in 1844 at Boston, Brownson attempted to examine the great social and political questions of the day in the light of religious principles. Thus, like Newman and the Oxford group, he became involved in the struggle of his age between intellectual liberalism and religious submissiveness. But unlike the more urbane Newman, the explosive Brownson gloried in pulverizing his opponents with his formidable logic. He was forced to suspend his periodical in 1864 because of ecclesiastical censure, and although it was revived in 1873, its final issue appeared in October 1875. Another attempt to maintain a really scholarly publication was made in later years in the case of the short-lived *New York Review,* a casualty of the Modernist scare, issued bi-monthly from St Joseph's Seminary, Dunwoodie, from 1905-1908, which proved as ill-fated as earlier American and English efforts.

Early magazines that survived and still flourish are the *Catholic World,* begun in 1865 by Father Isaac Hecker, founder of the Paulists, who also established the Catholic Publication Society, highly praised by the Second Plenary Council of Baltimore. The *Ave Maria,* a "family" magazine, was also started in 1865 by the Holy Cross priest, Edward Sorin, of Notre Dame. *America,* established in 1909 by the Society of Jesus as a weekly journal of opinion, soon earned an international reputation. It was followed in 1924 by the *Commonweal,* with Michael Williams as its first editor. A truly national organ, this review has long been recognized as an important voice of the intelligent Catholic layman on matters of world importance. Following World War II, the quarterly *Cross Currents,* devoted to "exploring the implications of Christianity for our times," was founded and has made available relevant articles by leading thinkers of the United States and Europe. Specialized periodicals likewise abound of which *Theological Studies, Theology Digest, Philosophy Today,* the *Catholic Historical Review,* the *Natural Law Review, Worship,* the *Ecumenist* and the *Bible Today* are but a few. University publications include *Thought,* the Fordham University quarterly, *Review of Politics* of the University of Notre Dame, and The Catholic University of America's several periodicals among which are the *American Ecclesiastical Review,* a highly-conservative monthly and the *Jurist,* a quarterly devoted to canon law.

Repeated efforts to form a Catholic Press Association finally took effect in 1911 at the national convention of the

American Federation of Catholic Societies in Columbus,
Ohio. The association now publishes a monthly bulletin, the
Catholic Journalist, and helps member-publications with
problems of circulation, advertising, typography, promoting,
editorial comment, etc. During its early years, the Catholic
Press Association organized a news service whereby member-
editors cooperated in the reporting and exchange of news.
But in 1920, the National Catholic Welfare Conference, recently organized, established its own News Service under the
auspices of the bishops, which superseded the prior arrangement of the association. Today the N.C.W.C. News Service
is probably the largest and most comprehensive Catholic
news agency in the world. Serving more than 150 Catholic
publications in the United States and Canada, with subscrib-
ing publications in sixty-three countries representing every
continent, the News Service gathers data through its numerous correspondents posted in the United States and throughout the world. Its excellent Rome Bureau transmits more
Vatican and other Catholic news than any other agency in
Rome.

Thus while fighting against great odds, American Catholic
newspapers and journals have slowly but surely increased
the range and power of the Catholic press in the United
States. After 140 years of trial and struggle, it now accurately
reflects both the strengths and weaknesses of American
Catholicism. While the number of diocesan weeklies has
grown to well over a hundred, and Catholic magazines at the
moment number more than 400, each commands a reader-
ship far smaller than one would hope for in a Catholic population of nearly forty-five million. Moreover, while the
growth in numbers speaks for itself, in the more difficult
achievement of quality and excellence no one will gainsay
the fact that these publications vary widely in terms of rele-
vancy and responsibility. But perhaps nothing is more indicative of the growing maturity of the Catholic press than the
fact that in many cases its editorials have changed from a
self-congratulatory tone to one that is more often self-critical,

even harshly so. This increased self-awareness of the Catholic press has raised certain issues in regard to the American Catholic press which apply to some extent also to that of the entire Anglo-Saxon world.

In the modern highly competitive world of journalism, the Catholic press no less than the secular press must face the question of rising costs, limited resources, and the proliferation of new periodicals. For better or worse, however, the Catholic press, unlike the general press, is not strictly subject to the normal economic forces that eliminate unfit publications. Subsidized by a religious Order or by charitable bequests, it is possible for a Catholic magazine to continue in publication even though it meet no special need or perform no special service. Thus while some of the best Catholic magazines are put out by religious Orders, so are some of the worst. Moreover, the alarming duplication of effort and needless competition for subscribers and advertisers, and even writers, create a situation which the Catholic community simply cannot afford. A serious depth study of the Catholic press as a whole in each of the English-speaking countries would provide guidelines for the major decisions regarding effective cooperation and even consolidation which may have to be made in the immediate future. It is clear that the deployment of men and resources in the Catholic press, as in education, will have to be more efficient in years to come, and the result may well be more emphasis on the needs to be met rather than on the freedom to publish regardless of need.

While defensive attitudes and parochialism were among the characteristics of the past of English-speaking Catholics, they are understandable only in the past. Unfortunately, however, their obtrusive influence is seen all too frequently in the Catholic press of our day. The belligerent stance which is assumed all too often whenever it is felt that non-Catholics may be in any way infringing on the rights of Catholics is a relic of the days when Catholics were made to feel that their faith barred them from full citizenship, but it has become anachronistic with the passage of years. Equally regrettable is the fact that so much of the Church's press still fails to meet the ultimate demands made upon any Catholic publication: to present the truth in a manner befitting that truth. The result is an adamant refusal to concede any Catholic wrong-doing or indeed any suggestion of differences of opinion among Catholics and an absurd sensitiveness to even reasonable criticism of the Church either from within or from without. As one American Lutheran minister remarked shortly after the presidential election of 1960, "It may be ridiculous to hold Senator Kennedy responsible for the St Bartholomew's Day Massacre and the Spanish Inquisition, yet so long as Catholics themselves fail to speak out in criticism of such events, they will remain as contemporary sins, unconfessed, unforgiven and for which penance is still required."

Another unfortunate consequence of the minority status of English-speaking Catholicism is the marked parochialism still reflected in so much of the Catholic press. While there are notable exceptions, most diocesan papers and national Catholic magazines show little concern for the pressing problems which confront the modern world, if one can judge by the space given to news accounts of these problems and editorial comments on them. All too rarely can one find intelligent coverage of such questions as the morality of nuclear warfare, the Christian obligation to aid the underdeveloped countries struggling towards a condition of full humanity, or the rôle of the United Nations, not to mention problems of national importance such as urban renewal and the incidence of racial and religious discrimination. The Church's universal character and mission demand a concern for the divine order as manifested on a world-wide scale which the Catholic press can and should foster in this generation of English-speaking Catholics who by family background and education are capable of much more sophisticated thinking than their immigrant forebears. A great disservice is done to the cause of mature and intelligent Catholicism when the Church's printed media tends to reduce refractory complexity to a manageable simplicity, and to project an inverted sense of values in its publications.

For as many years as it has been in operation, the Catholic press has had to grapple with the often delicate problem of its relationship to local ecclesiastical authority. There is, of course, no room to challenge the right and responsibility of bishops and major religious superiors to exercise vigilance concerning publications that bear the name of Catholic and for which the ultimate responsibility for orthodoxy of doctrine and the general norms of Christian morality and prudence rests with them. On the other hand, optimum freedom must be permitted if the editors and staff of such publications are to perform their professional tasks with the necessary competence. The history of Catholic journalism bears eloquent testimony to the tension that all too often exists between the two and which any period of crisis between Church and State, such as that involved in the school question, tends to aggravate. Happily, in our own day a partial solution to what no one will deny is a complex and difficult problem, is slowly evolving as exemplified by a recent announcement regarding one of the United States' oldest Catholic papers, and sixth largest in circulation. Bearing a new name and a new look, the February 28th, 1963, issue of the New Orleans *Clarion Herald* carried a statement by Archbishop John P. Cody regarding the paper's function. Making clear that he must hold himself responsible for a Catholic publication issued under his jurisdiction, the archbishop declared he did not intend the *Clarion Herald* to be thought of as a "house organ" nor as his "personal instrument". In fact, only those portions of the paper explicitly marked "official" should be taken as the Church's formal teaching. Otherwise, according to this prelate, the paper must also guard Catholic freedom and must not constrict the area of that freedom. Except when Catholic dogma is involved, it should also encourage and promote responsible discussion, and refrain from identifying any single viewpoint as the only orthodox belief.

Developments of this kind lend support to the hope that a real Catholic press is not completely outside the realm of possibility.

Because events of the past two decades during which the work of Pius XII, the renovation begun by John XXIII and his Vatican Council, and the advent of Paul VI have radically changed old attitudes towards Catholicism, the Church today as every publisher knows is "good copy." Thus incidents involving Catholic interests are given fairly wide coverage as well as editorial attention in both the secular and the religious press of the English-speaking world. As a consequence, it not infrequently happens that news stories in the secular press are at variance with accounts written exclusively for the Catholic press. Perhaps no more striking example of this can be cited than that furnished by the interesting ironies associated with the reporting on the first session of Vatican Council II. The first arises from the fact that the best reporting in the American press on the Council should have to appear in two *New Yorker* articles written under a pseudonym, thus bypassing the Catholic press and at least raising a question concerning the freedom enjoyed by Catholic publications. Another ironic development was the choice of Xavier Rynne by the Catholic Press Association of the United States for a special award for his "Letters from Vatican City" published in fall and winter (1962) issues of the *New Yorker*. For Xavier Rynne's success was the result of a simple decision to open up the Council to American readers despite the discipline of secrecy which seemingly was being observed more strictly in the Catholic English-speaking world than anywhere else. As Rynne pointed out, the articles were essentially collections of material supplied by the official press office of the Council and the ingenuity of individual reporters. As such, they were available to the American Catholic press representatives in Rome who, however, in their caution refused to use them.

In the case of the Council which was an event of tremendous significance for the entire world as well as for the

Church, accredited journalists of both secular and religious papers were merely fulfilling their professional duties in seeking to report the doings of the Council with completeness and honesty. It soon became evident that despite the bond of secrecy adopted by the Fathers of the Council, anyone with the requisite time, perseverance, and luck could find out almost everything that took place inside or on the periphery of the Council. If some of the reporting in the secular papers was faulty, it was more the result of lack of knowledge and perspective than prejudice or hostility. On the other hand, Catholic attempts to play down the clash of opinion between those of "liberal" and "conservative" persuasion among the more than 2,000 bishops in attendance can scarcely be justified. It is perhaps a sign of the times that Rynne's essay in what he called "theological journalism" was subsequently published in book form and is now in its fourth printing, with foreign rights already sold in England, Germany, France and Mexico. His greatest contribution may be one of the future, namely in the wholesome influence to be exercised on the Catholic press' coverage of the Council's second session. Europeans have long enjoyed a much greater freedom in airing their differences on subjects of Catholic interest than have their coreligionists of the English-speaking world. Whatever justification the past offers for this, today the unmistakable intellectual and cultural advance being made by English-speaking Catholics calls for a change in policy. While the level of performance of the latter may still be something less than spectacular, it would be naïve to attempt to perpetuate longer the cautious policy of shielding them from the knowledge of those events which, as a matter of record, are serving to make the Church better known and understood in our modern world.

CHAPTER V

CATHOLICISM AND NATIONAL LIFE AND CULTURE

With the exception of Ireland, Catholicism since the Reformation has not been something inherent in the way of life of the countries of the English-speaking world. On the contrary, down to the first part of the twentieth century, the established cultural pattern was not only alien to Catholicism, but Catholics in these countries were for the most part still resented and their Church suspect. As minority groups in nations which were first predominantly Protestant and later progressively secular in their culture, it is not surprising that they displayed many of the self-conscious attitudes so characteristic of such groups. Among these the tendency to withdraw into themselves and to assume the posture of defenders of a besieged fortress was probably the most serious because so contradictory of the Church's essentially universal mission.

Within the last few decades, however, the situation has vastly improved, and today Catholics are generally accepted as part of the national scene and the Church commands a more respectful hearing than ever before. These changed circumstances demand new qualities and an alteration in the kind of thinking that saw the Church through the difficult but comparatively less complicated past. Before considering some of the innumerable contemporary demands being made upon the Catholic body of the English-speaking world, a brief review of some of the formative influences of the past will be helpful and may serve to show that English-speaking Catholicism has more resources for the tasks ahead than are generally realized.

ENGLAND

While the complexity and nebulosity of the factors involved make generalizations more than ordinarily dangerous, even the most cautious would not deny that the history of English Catholicism in the nineteenth century exhibits two bewildering facts. On the one hand, there was the enormous growth of the Church, and on the other its almost complete lack of influence. This is explained in part by the fact that Catholic emancipation did not immediately erase the marks of three centuries of exclusion from the national life. Moreover, it came at a time when the advancing forces of liberal and secular rationalism not only made the conversion of England to Catholicism impossible, but even threatened the permanent survival of a dogmatic Christianity among the vast majority of the nation. In such a world Catholics were inevitably severed from the stream of national life as it flowed on from Protestantism to secularism.

The hope that the Oxford movement and the resultant impulse it gave to Catholicism in England might lead to a growth of the Church comparable to that which followed the missions of Augustine and Aidan, and that the new hierarchy would exercise a wide influence upon English life, proved altogether too optimistic. The English Catholic community certainly gained something in popular estimation from the fact that Newman, the greatest religious personality of the century, led the exodus of convert intellectuals from the Church of England. But with the complete rejection by the Archbishops of Canterbury and York of his fundamental contention regarding the nature of the Church, any possibility of Catholicizing the Established Church was doomed to failure. With the strong anti-Catholic reaction that inevitably followed, the majority of the Tractarians remained in the Anglican Church, too deeply rooted in her tradition and liturgy to take kindly to the new Roman devotions and religious practices which had such an appeal for men like Faber and Ward. It was unfortunate that at this particular time the communal liturgical worship of the Church was little practised or understood. Not until the twentieth century did the anti-Protestant conservatism of post-Tridentine Catholicism finally begin to yield to a wider, deeper, and more positive understanding and practice of the Catholic religion, though even today this movement is far from universal.

At the very time that the Anglicans were proclaiming their Protestantism in strident tones, the Catholic community in England was experiencing a phenomenal expansion from a quite disconnected source. Hundreds of thousands of Irish immigrants, driven from their homes by the potato famine, sought refuge in England where they created an immense Catholic democracy. But while the sheer weight of their numbers radically changed the proportional status of native English Catholics, the Irish added very little to Catholic intellectual life, and they had little or no voice in the direction of affairs in either the Church or the country. Not only did the leadership of the Catholic body remain overwhelmingly English, it showed no comprehension of the fact that the Catholic gentry were fast becoming only a small fraction of the laity. That it also showed even less understanding of the rôle of the laity is illustrated by the celebrated answer of Mgr George Talbot, the most influential Englishman in Rome in these years, to his own question: "What is the province of the laity? To hunt, to shoot, to entertain. These matters they understand, but to meddle with ecclesiastical matters they have no right at all . . ." It took generations of living together, as well as the coming of the welfare state and free education before this Irish immigrant class acquired a real influence in English Catholic affairs. By that time through long residence in England and intermarriage with the English, not to mention the gradual improvement of Anglo-Irish relations, Irish Catholics had grown less distinctively Irish and were mixing freely with those who had hitherto exercised a monopoly of influence. But it took another hundred years, despite Newman's "On Consulting the Faithful in Matters of Doctrine" which was first published in the *Rambler* for July 1859, before any effective steps were taken to restore the laity to their proper position within the Church.

In the history of the gradual evolution of an English Catholic democracy, the influence of Cardinal Manning, who became the head of the Church in England in 1865, was destined to be felt throughout the English-speaking world. From the outset of his episcopal career, Manning revealed a world-wide interest in social problems and tried to wean the Church in England from the cloister to public life, from the aristocratic to the democratic order. After his death his ideas lived on to the 1930's especially in the policies of one of his successors, Cardinal Hinsley, who openly declared Manning to be his model.

Manning's twenty-seven year rule at Westminster was a period of consolidation and ceaseless activity including his crusade for temperance, his championship of the cause of the working man and for land reform for the Irish, his support of the campaign against the white slave traffic, and his arbitration of the London dock strike of 1889. It was marred to some extent by his inflexible opposition to the proposed Oxford mission of Newman, his stubbornness in founding the University College at Kensington in 1874 which had such an unhappy history that, for better or worse, it seriously prejudiced any second attempt ever being made, and his unreasonable opposition to and dislike of religious Orders. In the long battle with the religious, the victory finally went to the bishops, and Manning was jubilant when in 1881 he learned that Leo XIII had issued the constitution *Romanos pontifices,* establishing full episcopal control over the missions of religious. The work Manning began was completed by the processes of time, and just as the converts, of whom there continued to be a thin but important stream, lost their direct dependence upon the Oxford movement, so too the Irish Catholics drifted from the self-conscious nationalism of the earlier immigrants. A new Catholic body resulted wherein the traditional ascendancy of the aristocracy was a thing of the past even as the destitution of the former immigrants no longer characterized those of Irish blood.

The cohesiveness of the Catholic body in England, however, was far from being monolithic in character. Except on questions of dogma, there was no obvious and single Catholic line, and in fact the record shows not only variety but inconsistency. In politics, for example, Catholics were found in every group from extreme Torys to left-wing Socialists, although few emerged as outstanding political leaders or statesmen. Those who became members of Parliament were indistinguishable from the non-Catholic members of their party or they did not remain long at Westminster. Even on national and international or colonial questions involving moral issues, there has seldom been a specifically Catholic reaction. In social groups, too, Catholics were absorbed by the English class structure and for the most part patterned their attitudes and behaviour on those of the class into which they were born or which they entered. In ecclesiastical matters such as liturgy, many different points of view prevailed.

The existence of this variety and freedom was, unfortunately, not recognized or understood by those outside the Church where it was increasingly evident that the intolerance of the past had been replaced by a widespread ignorance of Catholicism. Nor can it be denied that a large share of the responsibility for this must be attributed to the Catholics themselves. Despite the progress Catholicism had made, the net result failed to make an impact at the national level. All too many Englishmen saw only the externals of the beliefs and practices of their Catholic countrymen, and comprehended nothing of the doctrines on which they are based. Thus such Catholic practices as abstention from meat on Fridays, devotion to novenas, pilgrimages, and other activities that often give the impression of miracle-mongering, not to mention the Church's distinctive marriage laws, are often viewed as distasteful eccentricities.

On their side, Catholics have not been notably successful in communicating to the English public what English Catholicism really is. It is not without significance that while much of the great Newman's thought and writings were a distinct preparation for some of the most heartening of present-day developments, their full import was not understood or appreciated either inside or outside the Catholic Church of his day. Since the death of Newman, Catholic culture in the English-speaking world has known nothing to match the quality of his contributions. While later writers such as G. K. Chesterton, Christopher Dawson, Evelyn Waugh, and Graham Greene, who, incidentally, were all likewise converts, have had an impact on readers outside the Church, it remains to be seen how much of their work will prove of permanent service to English Catholicism. With a few exceptions, the record of achievement in theology, scripture, and philosophy was not impressive. Thus while the Church in England has been eminently successful in the task of ministering spiritually to its rapidly growing flock, in building churches and schools, and coping with the multitudinous problems of parochial life in large urban centres, it has not been as well equipped intellectually for the conditions of modern society or exercised the public influence proportionate to its numbers.

There is, however, another dimension to this problem of how far Catholicism can and should become a part of modern English culture. It touches on such sensitive areas of traditional Catholic teaching as sexual morality, marriage and divorce, education and censorship, and the relationship of Church and State which are at variance with those held by the majority of the English people. These are real differences and will probably remain so, but since in our modern pluralistic society all groups enjoy the benefits of freedom of conscience, Catholics can hardly deny them to others even if they were in a position to do so. Hence, Catholics, while maintaining their own position on basic questions of belief, would do well to make it clear that they do not seek to dictate to those who do not share the Catholic faith, but only to offer a full and candid elucidation to those who are willing to listen.

The universal acclaim accorded to the late Pope John XXIII's encyclical, *Pacem in Terris*, furnished a dramatic proof of the fact that it is possible for Catholics to speak, in fidelity to their own traditions, to those outside the Church and to make an impact of great importance for the Church and the world. If in the past, Catholic leaders, both clerical and lay, were otherwise too engaged to manifest much concern for any but the narrow interests of the Catholic body itself, such a course of action can no longer be justified. Today's world offers both the challenge and the opportunity for Catholics to work together with their fellow citizens in searching out answers to such complex questions as nuclear warfare, international organization, the population problem, racial relations, and a host of other issues which press more and more insistently for solution.

SCOTLAND

In Scotland where the growth and expansion of Catholicism since emancipation has been solid if not spectacular, the Education Act of 1918, already discussed, was an event of great importance in the history of the relations of the Catholic community to the national life and culture. It not only brought immediate financial relief to Scottish Catholics, but it helped their integration into the national life to an extent hitherto impossible. This Scottish solution of a difficulty which is endemic to modern national life has worked harmoniously for nearly half a century to the great benefit of Church and country. With better educational opportunities available, Scottish Catholics made ever-increasing contributions to the national life, particularly in literature, radio, fine arts, and the professions, although that contribution is still not proportionate to their numbers. Nevertheless, the influence of the work of such men as Fion Mac Colla, Moray MacLaren, Sir Compton Mackenzie, Colm Brogan, Bruce Marshall, and George Scott-Moncrieff has been far from negligible. The passage of the Roman Catholic Relief Bill in 1926 removed practically all the anti-Catholic legislation which had survived since emancipation and henceforth Catholics were assured the legal right to have a bell and steeple on their places of worship, the clergy were permitted to wear religious habits and vestments in public and to hold property as corporate bodies, while Catholic charities were granted exemption from income tax and other dues, previously granted only to non-Catholic charities.

With the disappearance of these cruder expressions of intolerance and the increased participation of Catholics in the general life of the nation, a friendlier interest in the Catholic Church gradually emerged. For the first time since the sixteenth century, Scottish students of history, art, literature, and politics looked for their inspiration to the literature and achievements of pre-Reformation Scotland. A revival of interest in Gaelic culture likewise resulted in a growing appreciation of the Catholic Church. Through local and national politics, Catholics attained various positions of importance. The important city of Glasgow had a Catholic Lord Provost from 1938 to 1941, and each parliament has included a few Catholic members. Despite these encouraging signs, it will take many more years before the inbred hostility to Catholicism has fully disappeared from Scotland and Catholics are completely accepted for what they are. Meanwhile, perhaps the most important development is that taking place within the Scottish Catholic community itself where the mentality which felt itself inferior and instinctively anticipated bigotry is yielding to a more mature sense of confidence and an easier assumption of its rightful place in the community.

WALES

As we have already seen, the progress of the Catholic Church in Wales since the Reformation, has been slow and incredibly difficult. With the great influx of Irish into South Wales in the mid-nineteenth century, the struggle of clergy and laity alike was to provide for the needs of the immigrants amid a very hostile environment. Given the almost completely foreign cast of the Catholic Church, it is not surprising that it has exercised almost no influence in national life and culture. The situation has not been improved by the fact that Catholics have played little or no part in the movement, which received a strong impetus after World War II, to halt the impoverishment of national culture by restoring the Welsh language as the medium of instruction in public schools. In very recent times, a small beginning was made in the work of such organizations as *Y Cych Catholig* (Catholic Circle) and a group of scholars from *An Réalt,* the Irish-speaking praesidium of the Legion of Mary, whose programmes include the use of the Welsh language and the sponsorship of a growing number of Welsh publications of devotional and theological import. However, there is as yet no overall approach to the problem, nor even a seminary specifically equipped to deal with Welsh religious vocations so that aspirants to the priesthood would no longer be forced to go to European seminaries, thereby cutting themselves off from their national ethos.

IRELAND

In the Republic of Ireland, the place of religion in national life and culture was expressly provided for in the Constitution adopted in 1937. That instrument not only ordains that religion shall be honoured and respected in the country, but it also recognizes the special position of the Catholic

Church as the guardian of the faith professed by the great majority of the citizens. Freedom of conscience and the free profession and practice of religion are, however, guaranteed to all citizens, and the government is prohibited from endowing any religion or discriminating on the basis of religious belief or practice. Thus the legal position of the Church in Ireland is unique among the English-speaking countries of the world. Although its intellectual achievements in modern times have not been great, the world is enormously indebted to Irish Catholicism for its missionary zeal and accomplishments. Moreover, more recently Ireland has given an example to the world by the increasingly responsible rôle its representatives have played in the United Nations. In commending the Irish for this on the occasion of his visit in May 1963, to Dublin, President Kennedy pointed out that the peacekeeping machinery of the United Nations cannot work without the help of the smaller nations—nations whose forces threaten no one and whose forces can thus help create a world where no nation is threatened by force.

The problem of the partition of Ireland between the Irish Republic and Northern Ireland though still not resolved after more than forty years, no longer generates the rancour of earlier years. Nevertheless, the Catholics of the North have felt discriminated against by the Belfast government in matters like education and public employment, while the Protestants of the North do not take kindly to the legislation on divorce and the censorship of literature and films of the Dublin government. A recent proposal looking to a solution of this problem of partition suggested that the first step must be a public declaration that the Irish government will not attempt in any way, either by force or propaganda, to change the situation in the Six Counties without the agreement of a majority of the people in the area. Thus if a majority in Northern Ireland should come to seek union with the rest of Ireland, they should be allowed to do so on terms of their own choosing.

AUSTRALIA AND NEW ZEALAND

One of the most interesting features of the Catholic history of Australia and New Zealand is the prominent part played by the Church in the formation of a programme of radical social action and the establishment of the principle of State secularity. The struggle of John Therry, the Irish missionary to the Antipodes, was the first phase of the battle against an established church and for the improvement of social conditions for the poor. Therry's ten-year fight in the 1820's against State endowment of the Church of England in New South Wales was successful and set a pattern which the Catholic minority of Australia has always insisted upon as a guarantee against all forms of Protestant ascendancy. His work on behalf of the convicts who were victims of the frightful abuses and brutalities of the penal system and the assignment system associated with it made him the forerunner of the Catholic social movement.

The social movement among Australia's Catholics stemmed not only from the Irish revolt against Protestant-British ascendancy, but also from the social experiences of the immigrants in their new country where they were among the poorest and most under-privileged. Under the leadership of their clergy, these pioneer reformers, including the valiant Caroline Chisholm, launched and carried forward a crusade which transcended all distinctions of creed. During the second half of the nineteenth century, Catholics continued to play a leading part in social reform aligning themselves with land reform groups and the rank and file of the new labour union movement, of which they became the leaders after World War I.

Despite this identification of the Church with the social planning and social welfare policies which are such a unique mark of Australian life and culture, the deep prejudices against Catholicism derived from the past retained their force even though they were not as openly expressed as formerly. Catholic and Irish stood out against Protestant and English, and little was done to bridge the gap between them. Even today when the immigrants from Europe have changed the exclusively Irish character of the Catholic body and the very celebration of St Patrick's Day has become more and more of an empty formality, the thought of many non-Catholic Australians has not yet adjusted to the actualities of the new situation. Moreover, times have changed with respect to Catholic power in politics since the days when the Irish issue dominated the scene. In recent years Catholics no longer have concentrated almost entirely in the Labour Party which previously enabled them to hold important offices in the government. As a consequence of the split during the 1950's in both the Labour Party and the Catholic vote, the influence of Catholics in public life has been greatly diminished. Since the power exercised by Catholics of leftist sympathies in politics and labour unions undoubtedly contributed to the distrust and prejudice against Catholicism, this "depoliticizing" of Catholic life has had its advantages.

Up to thirty years ago, Catholic colleges at the universities were definitely outsiders with little or no influence on intellectual life. Today more cordial relations exist between the authorities of Catholic and Anglican colleges in some parts of the country and are expressive of the new ecumenical spirit in Australia. The uncritical attitude of the past towards immigration and the "White Australia" policy is likewise at present being questioned by a growing number of Australians, including many Catholics. Led by an organization formed in 1961, the Immigration Reform Association, active groups in the six States of the country have urged a more flexible approach. Their arguments echo much of what the Australian Catholic hierarchy have for some years been saying with respect to the immorality of the colour bar, the disastrous effect Australia's racial discrimination has had on non-European world opinion, and the benefits that Asian and non-European immigration can bring to the country, provided it is regulated according to Australia's economic need. These represent small but hopeful beginnings of a change in what has been the traditional policy of Australian Catholics who have concerned themselves almost exclusively with extending their plant and building their defences. While they have at times also exercised a powerful influence in the social and political field, this has all too often aroused distrust as "alien," instead of proving a leavening influence in national life and thought. Present trends indicate a growing awareness on the part of Australia's Catholic body that the nineteenth-century isolationist mentality which alienated it from its fellow citizens and made it insensitive to the needs of the rest of the world, is out of harmony with the movement of the Church universal.

SOUTH AFRICA

In South Africa, as we have seen, out of a total population of about sixteen million, a small minority of about five million Whites, of whom only a small percentage are Catholic, are in complete and thorough ascendancy, politically, educationally, economically, and socially. The policy of segregation or *apartheid* as a means of maintaining this White supremacy has the full support of the Dutch Reformed Church to which the majority of the ruling class belong. To this end, South Africa is rich in laws enabling the government to prevent agitation of any kind against its *apartheid* policies. These include the Criminal Laws Amendment Act, the Riotous Assemblies Act, the Public Safety Act, the Suppression of Communism Act, and the General Law Amendment Act of 1962. Such a multiplicity of laws seems unnecessary when Communism is legally defined as "Any doctrine or scheme which aims at bringing about any political, industrial, social, or economic change within the Union by the promotion of disturbance or disorder, by unlawful acts or omissions, or by threats of such acts or omissions." The most recent act suspended the right of *habeas corpus* and has earned the title of the "No Trial Bill". Its inspiration apparently resulted from an official inquiry into the activities of a secret organization known as Poqo, a name meaning something like Sinn Fein.

In South Africa's tragic circumstances, the position of the Catholic Church could scarcely be more perilous. Nevertheless, despite reprisals, the Church continues to speak out in support of racial unity.

CANADA

By authority of the British North America Act of 1867 under which the dominion was erected, Canada is a two-culture country. Language, history, and geography have served to associate the Catholic Church more closely with the French who constitute about two-thirds of the total Catholic population of Canada. The dominance of the French element remained even when large post-World War II immigration brought an increase in the number of non-French Catholics to Canada, including Italians, Poles, and Ukrainians, as well as English and Irish, raising the Catholic population of Canada to about forty-five per cent of the total. By reason of the adherence of the French Catholics to a language and cultural pattern different from that of the Anglo-Saxon majority, the Church has experienced a considerable degree of isolation in some of the provinces. On the contrary, nowhere on the continent have the affairs of Church and State been so intermingled, especially in the areas of culture and education, as in Quebec. For centuries that province has had a Catholic system of public education which, up to very recent times, provided terminal training for those not going on to university studies. Complementing the public system, are a large number of "Collèges Classiques" maintained for the most part by religious Orders which provide the preparatory training for those destined to become French Canada's intellectuals, professional men and churchmen.

In making provision for those Canadian Catholics who

were not French by descent and language and who were scattered throughout the predominantly Protestant sections of the country, the Church's efforts were made easier by the growing economic development and expansion of the country, in which all alike were interested, which militated against discriminatory religious policies even in the provinces in which Catholics formed a small minority. Nevertheless, it is still sufficiently rare for a Canadian Catholic to reach high academic position outside the great French-Canadian Catholic universities, that the recent appointment of Dr John Francis Leddy as President of the non-denominational University of Windsor at Windsor, Ontario, gave more than ordinary satisfaction to his coreligionists. This appointment was generally regarded as a considerable step forward in the recognition of Catholic scholarship in English-speaking Canada.

THE UNITED STATES

Historically speaking, the Protestantism which was brought to North America in the two-pronged colonization begun at Jamestown in 1607 and Plymouth in 1620 became normative in the national life and culture of what finally came to be known as the United States. From the seventeenth to the mid-twentieth century this version of Christianity, which was of British more than continental provenance and was identified not with any one of the multiplying denominations but with Protestantism as a whole, constituted what has been called the country's "only national religion". During this period, to be an American normally meant to be a Protestant—this was the religious identification that in the American mind quite naturally went along with being an American. That non-Protestants felt the force of this conviction almost as strongly as did the Protestants was evidenced by the development of separate sub-cultures or associations as in the proverbial Catholic or Jewish "ghettos". Within the past generation the picture has been so radically transformed that now terms such as "pluralist" and "post-Protestant" are used to describe the new situation in which Protestantism is but one of three different forms of being religious in the American way. Today, not only Protestants, but increasingly Catholics and Jews as well, are accepted as Americans not apart from, or in spite of, their religion, but because of it. Before examining the implications of this change for American Catholicism, it will be helpful to review briefly its status during the more than three centuries when the American Protestant ethos was dominant.

Despite the intense and persistent antagonism to the Catholic Church which the English colonists brought to America in the seventeenth century, and which struck such enduring roots that it became one of the major traditions of their subsequent history, the dawn of independence brought to Bishop Carroll's little flock the distinction of being the first Catholic minority to enjoy political freedom in the modern English-speaking world. Though small in size, this Catholic community was well-established and secure in social position, counting among its communicants some of the wealthiest merchants and planters in the country. Had this small aristocratic Anglo-American group of the early years not been overshadowed by the large numbers of non-English immigrants, the rôle played by Catholicism in the life and culture of the nation might well have been a more positive one. What actually happened is well known: the Catholic body in the United States was increased by the large numbers of Irish and German immigrants who began arriving in the middle decades of the nineteenth century, and towards the close of the century, by the great tide of immigration from central and southern Europe.

The herculean task of providing a Catholic setting for these immigrants was made more difficult by the native opposition which arose outside the Church, and the deep rifts which developed within it between those of dissimilar cultures. If the intellectual and cultural accomplishments of the Catholic group were in no way impressive during these years of numerical growth, it is not surprising considering the pov-

erty and low social standing of most of the newcomers. Moreover, all the energies of the American clergy and hierarchy
were necessarily absorbed in the immediate task of preserving the religious faith of the immigrants, assisting them to
adjust to the strange environment, and protecting them from
the strident attacks of the nativists. The success of these efforts, while not accomplished without numerous crises and
setbacks, has been recorded by the non-Catholic historian,
Henry Steele Commager, who wrote: "It might, indeed, be
maintained that the Catholic Church was, during this period,
[since 1880] one of the most effective of all agencies for
democracy and Americanization".

One of the crises within the Catholic minority at the turn
of the century concerned the extent to which traditional
Catholic practices should be adapted to the American milieu.
The broad approach of men like Gibbons, Ireland, and
Keane in trying to relate Catholicism to the secular society of
the United States was looked upon with suspicion by the
more conservative members of the hierarchy led by Archbishop Michael A. Corrigan of New York who feared such
efforts would imperil the integrity of Catholic doctrine. A
heated controversy developed when a French translation of
Walter Elliott's *Life of Father Hecker* led to an exaggerated
interpretation of the Paulist's ascetical principles and apolo-
getical practices which together with certain statements of
Ireland and the other liberals of the American Church were
grouped together under the term "Americanism". When Leo
XIII in his papal letter *Testem benevolentiae* of January
22nd, 1899, summarized certain false doctrines which were
imputed to some within the American Church through the
translation of a book in a foreign tongue, he was at pains
to make clear he was not condemning those laudable political
and social qualities of the American people which were also
sometimes called "Americanism". While the more conservative prelates in the United States thanked the pope for saving
the American Church from the danger of heresy, the fol-
lowers of Gibbons maintained that no American Catholic

held the condemned doctrines and that the errors which had acquired the name of Americanism were caricatures of the real ideas of Fr Hecker and of American Catholicism as it actually existed.

This condemnation, and that of modernism in the next decade, undoubtedly helped to account for the fact that until quite recently the American Church has been less concerned with theological, philosophical and speculative thought in general than have the Catholics of England, Germany, or France. Moreover, it now appears that the pressing necessities of proving that Catholics could be good Americans may perhaps have resulted in a too hasty Americanization to the detriment of the pluralistic linguistic and cultural contributions which the Catholic immigrant groups could have made to the enrichment of American life. Whatever the deficiencies and even mistakes of these years, they in no way denigrate the very real achievements of this immigrant age when millions of Catholics of divergent origin and background arrived in the United States in the century beginning in 1820 and were encouraged by their new spiritual leaders to amalgamate and adapt themselves to ideals which were both American and Catholic. If, however, the circumstances of the past account in part for the lack of American Catholic intellectual achievement and for the paucity of Catholics in posts of national influence and leadership, the present position of the Church in the United States demands a more mature response to the complex problems of contemporary society.

For the first time in their history, the Catholics of the United States, while still a minority, are no longer a beleaguered one. The decline in immigration which relieved the Church of what had been its most important task, protecting and training the immigrants, also marked the beginning of a change in the isolation or separateness which had served some interests during the earlier period. Today the Church in the United States has emerged from the catacombs and is in every way more respectable intellectually, socially, and economically than it was a generation ago. While it is true that evidences of old wounds still persist, and there are still places where Catholics are not welcome, these instances are more and more the exception. This changed historical situation has encouraged the hope that the next generation may penetrate more deeply and influence more widely the total secular society of the country. In some respects, the tasks ahead present more of a challenge than anything hitherto experienced. There is considerable evidence at hand which suggests that what has been called the secularization of our culture will probably continue, that the vestigial religious elements which have been carried along out of the past for some generations now without roots of their own, will become less and less effective in ordering men's lives. Nevertheless, in numerous areas of contemporary society, both within the Catholic Church and outside, and both in the United States and throughout the English-speaking world, there are promising signs of progress in relations between Catholics and those of other religious faiths, of which the following few examples will serve as illustrations.

The advantages that have come to the Church in the English-speaking world from living and growing in an atmosphere of religious and political freedom have been repeatedly acknowledged and unreservedly endorsed by American Catholic leaders from John Carroll on. Nevertheless, a doubt persists in the minds even of sincere and fair-minded non-Catholics regarding the official position of the Catholic Church on religious toleration and the relations of Church and State. Moreover, the record of history supplies them with evidence of many faults committed by and in the Catholic Church against freedom of conscience. Among the many heartening developments of the past year, however, the statement on the principle of religious freedom by Cardinal Bea, President of the Secretariat for Promoting Christian Unity, is significant of the change taking place even at Rome in regard to this opinion. According to the cardinal,

This freedom consists in man's right to decide perfectly freely on his own destiny in accordance with his own conscience. Out of this freedom spring the duty and the right of man to follow his own conscience. Corresponding to this right and duty there is the duty of the individual and of society to respect this freedom and self-determination.

In preparation for the last session of Vatican Council II, a schema on religious freedom had been prepared by the Secretariat. Furthermore, this teaching was confirmed by the late Pope John XXIII himself in his encyclical, *Pacem in Terris*, which stated: "Every human being has the right to honour God according to the dictates of an upright conscience and, therefore, the right to worship God privately and publicly." Both inside and outside the Church there is hope that action by the Council on the issue of religious freedom will serve to dissipate once and for all the misconceptions that have divided Christians for more than four centuries. Among the suggestions put forward by Fr Hans Küng, the Tübingen theologian who is one of the Council "experts," during his lecture-tour in the United States in the spring of 1963, were a number of very practical measures related to this subject.

Another trend representative of the changed temper of our times is the increasing emphasis on the position and function of the layman in the life of the Church. During the nineteenth and early decades of the twentieth century, forces were at work which greatly diminished the impetus towards free expression by the laity as members of the Church and as American citizens. Recent developments in the life of the Church itself and in contemporary society have acted to change this situation. In the last few years, many bishops in the United States and Canada, for example, have appointed laymen to diocesan school boards, ecumenical commissions, and liturgical committees. A number of the hierarchy have already announced that the laity will play a part in the diocesan synods to be held after Vatican II finishes its work so that local customs and regulations dealing with marriage ceremonies, liturgy, etc., may be brought into line with the spirit and letter of the ecumenical council.

In April 1963 Cardinal Cushing of Boston addressed a

pastoral letter on certain aspects of this problem of lay co-re-
sponsibility to the clergy and faithful of his archdiocese and
"to men of good will in every tradition". Specifically, the letter treated of the layman's responsibility to contribute to an
informed public opinion in the Church. "The very structure
of the Church," the cardinal noted, "suggests that public-
opinion is an essential part of its existence as an institution".
Recognizing that it is never easy to maintain the balance
between authority and freedom, and that the obligation to
preserve without change essential Christian doctrine rests
upon the bishops, Cardinal Cushing nevertheless stoutly af-
firmed that the first function of authority in the Church is
not to bind the human spirit or to narrow the area of knowledge, but "to open gates which lead into new ways". In words
splendidly reminiscent of John XXIII, he urged: "Far better
to tolerate some small indiscretion in the expression of public
opinion than to discourage legitimate views and deprive the
Church of that leaven which may invigorate the whole body".

It is not far-fetched to conclude that these stirrings are an
expression of the new Catholic consciousness which has
gripped the Church since Vatican Council II. This latter
was described by Hans Küng as: "joy in the new freedom,
the new possibilities, the new initiatives within the Catholic
sphere and in the relations with other Christian communi-
ties; joy in the renewal which has become possible within
the Church as a preparation for the reunion of divided Christians". If this movement for unity took longer in starting in
the English-speaking world than it did in Central Europe
where there has been a long tradition of ecumenical encoun-
ter, it is, as we shall now see, making very gratifying progress.

CHAPTER VI

QUEST FOR UNITY

Of the many gratifying dimensions of modern Christianity, the movement toward unity which has steadily been gathering momentum since the beginning of this century is perhaps the most striking and far-reaching in its consequences. With the rapid increase of world population, Christians faced the fact that by the mid-twentieth century they were a mere fraction of mankind and possibly destined to become an even smaller one. The bewildering variety of sects, frequently divided on minute points of theology with a European background and with no meaning in the Asian or African context, resulted in a weakening of the witness of the Christian Gospel, if not outright scandal, in the eyes of the world. Given these facts, and the growing menace of secularism and irreligion, concern over the problem of Christian disunity took on a new sense and note of urgency which was not without consequences in the English-speaking world.

Long years of preparation among the major Episcopalian and Protestant bodies resulted, in 1948, in the coming together of 170 different Churches to form the World Council of Churches, the precise aim of which was the achievement of unity of belief and ministry among Christians. The serious theological inquiries which have characterized so much of the Council's work have generally resulted in a new confrontation with the faith as preserved by the Roman Catholic and Orthodox communions. For example, their study of the complex problem of religious liberty and Christian witness led, curiously enough, to the publication of a study (by a Spanish ex-Jesuit who is now a Protestant minister) called *Roman Catholicism and Religious Liberty* in which Catholic literature on the subject was examined and the conclusion reached that the overwhelming majority of contemporary authors are, generally speaking, in doctrinal accord with Protestant ecumenical statements on religious liberty.

The impact of the ecumenical movement varied, however, in different parts of Christendom, as did official and unofficial Catholic reaction to it. In regard to the separated Eastern Churches, Rome favoured the ecumenical approach of negotiating with the patriarchs and bishops in the hope of preparing an ecclesiastical reconciliation, and has, therefore, never encouraged individual conversions. In regard to Protestant Christians, Catholic ecumenism developed more rapidly in the countries of Europe where the Catholic Church faced a fairly homogeneous community of Protestants committed to a traditional creed, a liturgy, and a common theological tradition. Thus in Germany, for example, where theologians have been meeting since 1946, an "astonishingly far-reaching agreement between contemporary Roman Catholic and Evangelical scholarship" has been reached in the area of biblical studies according to Edmund Schlink, the Heidelberg professor who is one of the Protestant observers at Vatican Council II. Real differences remain in the area of dogma although here, too, certain areas of agreement were discovered. The German experience has served to emphasize the truth of Schlink's statement that while "the union of separated Churches cannot be achieved through scholarly work . . . just as certainly it cannot come to be without this work". In English-speaking countries, on the other hand, Catholics until recently remained little impressed with ecumenism, largely because the great variety of Protestant traditions which they encountered led them to concentrate their efforts principally on the work of individual conversions.

The growing importance of the ecumenical movement and the increasing desire of Catholics to participate in it led the Holy Office in December 1949 to issue a somewhat aus-

tere instruction designed to guide Catholics on the proper
conduct of ecumenical encounters. So rigorously were the
prohibitions against religious cooperation with non-Catholics
observed in the English-speaking world, however, that even
such a generous initiative as Cardinal Hinsley's "Sword of
the Spirit" movement fell into unexpected difficulties after
his death. Founded in 1940 to encourage joint action among
Christians in the field of social and international justice, it
became a purely Catholic organization with much narrower
aims. This spirit of conservatism and suspicion marked the
response not only to the ecumenical movement itself, but to
the allied liturgical and biblical revivals as well, and was generally characteristic of Anglo-American Catholicism.

Despite this generally hostile climate, England and America have had their share of individuals who have tried to free
Catholics from the inhibiting effects of the polemics of the
Counter-Reformation. Writing of the Lambeth Conference
of 1920 from which issued the "Life and Work" and "Faith
and Order" movements, precursors of the World Council of
Churches, the English Dominican, Vincent McNabb, looked
forward to the day when the pope might welcome an Archbishop of Canterbury in a gesture of charity which would be
a pledge of future reconciliation. Seemingly an impossible
hope at the time, it has actually come to pass in little more
than a generation. Moreover, long before such gatherings
had become common, theological discussions between Catholics and non-Catholics were arranged regularly by the convert Dominican priest, Henry St John, and met alternately
at a Dominican priory and at the mother house of the Anglican community of the Resurrection. Concerned less with
argument than the interpretation of each other's minds, the
conferences resulted in a growing understanding and appreciation of differing points of view. The participation of the
Abbot of Downside, Dom Basil Christopher Butler, a distinguished biblical scholar, and Mgr Francis Davis, the vice-
postulator for the cause of beatification of Cardinal Newman
and a pioneer in teaching theology in non-Catholic univer-

sities, to mention just two, contributed to improving relations between Christians in England at an informed theological level.

In the United States the Protestant-Catholic dialogue, for a variety of reasons, took longer in getting under way and the number of men who actually talked with one another for a sustained period of time on central ecumenical problems was never large. Indeed, for years the burden was borne by a handful of men—pioneers whose own interest and intensity were in contrast to a suspicion and apathy. Even today, the attitude towards ecumenical dialogue differs radically from diocese to diocese. Some ordinaries and superiors are very permissive in allowing priests and laymen to take part in interfaith programmes, while in the case of others the opposite is true. However, the providential impetus given to the movement in recent years by Pope John XXIII gives rise to the hope that the future will find the Catholic ecumenical thrust so firmly established throughout the Anglo-American world that a hesitant bishop will find himself clearly going against the current of the Church.

Although it would not be proper to credit John XXIII alone with the creation of the present surge of ecumenical interest in Catholic circles, what he did that was so important was to give his blessing to the ecumenical forces already tentatively at work within the Roman Catholic Church. His encouragement and support made ecumenical-minded Catholics realize that they were not merely being tolerated, that they were not merely fringe voices, but were articulating those emphases that the Holy Father wished to have at the centre of the Church's life and concern. To this end, the creation of the Secretariat for Promoting Christian Unity as a permanent organization within the Church may well stand as equally important with any accomplishment of Vatican Council II. With the creation of the Secretariat, a structure was provided wherein Catholic theologians might speak through and for the Church and not just for themselves.

But if the structure was important as a symbol of a revolutionary change, the spirit behind its creation was even more significant. Pope John's inflection of the phrase "separated brethren," with the noun receiving more emphasis than the adjective, highlighted a neglected aspect in Catholic thought, namely, the conviction that any baptized Christian is in some sense, by virtue of his baptism, joined already into the Mystical Body of Christ which is his Church. Moreover, the pope's sensitivity to his fellow men and his desire that the Church should move away from past controversies into a new kind of relationship with all non-Catholics found many other forms of expression among which the removal from the Good Friday Liturgy of the phrase usually translated as "perfidious Jews," and the warm welcome extended to Archbishop Geoffrey Fisher of Canterbury and the Moderator of the Church of Scotland were typical. For the first time, too, five Catholic theologians acting as official observers for the Vatican attended the Third Assembly of the World Council of Churches held in 1961 in New Delhi, India.

Such leads as these inspired many local attempts to improve relations between Catholics and other citizens with the result that, while old animosities no doubt remain on the fringe, in the central dialogue of the communions they are giving way to an active restoration of brotherly love. On all sides, care is now taken to avoid discourtesy, to express profound differences with charity and understanding, to discuss divergences with obvious respect for one another's point of view, and to eschew at all costs judgments on others' sincerity and truth. Thus an entirely new climate has been created which, for Catholics and non-Catholics alike means a dramatic break with the attitudes of the past.

Although the change in the ecumenical climate that followed the calling of Vatican Council II found Catholics in the Anglo-American world largely unprepared, the earlier informal contacts soon bore fruit. In the course of 1962 at least four important ecumenical gatherings were held in England, the most significant perhaps being the Heythrop Conference called by the Christian Unity Committee of the English hierarchy. Presided over by Cardinal Bea, who was paying his first visit to England, this gathering was concerned with instructing members of the clergy themselves in the true meaning of the ecumenical apostolate. It proved a milestone in the history of Catholic ecumenical work in England and provided concrete evidence of the new determination to exchange polemics for understanding and the pursuit of truth through charity. In the other three gatherings Catholic and non-Catholic theologians discussed specific themes, perhaps the most significant being the Mirfield conference on the apostolic constitution of the Church. In each case the presence of continental theologians resulted in exchanges which were valuable in terms of international understanding as well as in their primary religious context.

If memories of the Malines Conversations of forty years ago when Anglicans and Belgian and French Catholic theologians met to discuss what was in those days called "reunion," and reports of contemporary contacts between continental Catholic scholars and Anglican theologians sometimes cause confusion and anxiety to English Catholics whose sense of propriety and piety, not to mention inner security, seems threatened, this is not surprising. For some Christians the ecumenical movement, even as exemplified in the Secretariat for Promoting Christian Unity, appears to be encouraging what an English Dominican described as "a kind of indifferentism . . . concerning the uniqueness of the one true Church as the way of salvation for all men and so hindering individual conversions." In part, the misunderstanding behind this anxiety stems merely from the shock of hearing in public some obvious yet unfamiliar truths, as for example when Archbishop Heenan of Liverpool (since promoted to Westminster) told a mixed audience in Northern Ireland in July, 1962 that "being a Christian is more important than being a Catholic or a Protestant". This stress on the supreme importance of incorporation in Christ by grace does not depreciate the importance of being a member, in the full sense, of the Catholic Church. Yet it is a fact that the winds of change are at work in contemporary Catholicism. However, as long as it is clear, as Australian Bishop Bryan Gallagher recently noted, that "any unity of the Churches achieved by bargaining, compromise or by soft-peddling unresolved differences would be spurious," no Catholic need fear. For true ecumenism is the very opposite of indifferentism and exists only where men share a burning conviction that religious belief and unity are matters of supreme importance.

In North America, likewise, the ecumenical awakening made remarkable progress in a very short time. Countless discussion and working groups were formed throughout the continent which made possible new contacts between Catholic, Protestant, and Orthodox Christians, both theologians and laymen, and between Christians and Jews. A growing number of publications including the specialized theological periodical, *Journal of Ecumenical Studies*, were indicative of the spreading interest in ecumenical theology. Among other heartening signs were the programmes of graduate studies in theology, with appropriate degrees, which were introduced in Catholic institutions such as Notre Dame, Marquette, and the University of San Francisco as a response to the new interest of lay people in this area.

The four-day Roman Catholic-Protestant Colloquium held at Harvard University from March 27th to March 30th, 1963, must also be recorded as an important milestone in ecumenical history. Its importance was heightened by the appearance of the eighty-one-year-old Cardinal Bea for a series of three lectures on the Council and Christian unity. While the founding fathers of the Massachusetts Bay Colony would undoubtedly have been scandalized at the sight of a cardinal of Rome in a place of honour on a Harvard stage, and while many Catholics would probably still reciprocate, the fact that these meetings took place at all, and took place where they did, is evidence of how fully the quest for Christian understanding has entered into the mainstream of American religious life.

Recent years have also seen a rapid growth of ecumenical activity in Canada. With the approval of Cardinal Léger,

Archbishop of Montreal, a French-speaking Protestant-Catholic dialogue was inaugurated in October 1958 with a gathering at the Jesuit Collège Ste Marie, since which the group has met regularly with great profit. In 1959 an ecumenical group of English-speaking clergymen was formed, composed of Catholic theologians and professors of the Protestant Faculty of Divinity of McGill University. Their meetings, which have been held regularly, have attracted an increasing number of representatives of the Protestant, Catholic, and Orthodox communions. Joint meetings of the two groups took place during the Christian Unity Octave in 1961 and 1962 and featured brief addresses in French and English, the reading of extracts from Holy Scripture having to do with unity, and the singing of psalms and recitation of prayers together.

The movement received fresh impetus with the accession of John XXIII and the creation of the Secretariat for Promoting Christian Unity. Cardinal Léger, already greatly interested, created an archdiocesan ecumenical commission in Montreal whose objective was to maintain and further existing relationships, to establish new ones, to combat prejudice, and to educate Catholics so as to bring about more intelligent and harmonious relations with Christians belonging to other Churches, and with non-Christians. Of the nine members of this archdiocesan commission, two were laymen. In recognition of the fact that while doctrinal problems are best left to specialists in theology, the initiative of laymen and their involvement in ecumenism is extremely important, the commission sponsored an introductory course of lectures on ecumenism open to Catholics and non-Catholics which aroused great interest.

Montreal's interest in and record of ecumenical activity were no doubt factors in the choice of that predominantly Catholic city for the Fourth World Conference on Faith and Order which was held from July 12th to July 26th, 1963, at McGill University. As a department within the World Council of Churches, Faith and Order is concerned with sacrament, order, and doctrine and for that reason has been the centre for the greatest Christian activity in theology and liturgy. Greater representation and more active participation by Orthodox and Catholic spokesmen contributed both to the success and frustration of the Montreal conference. The Third Assembly of Faith and Order at Lund, Sweden, in 1952, was largely an inter-Protestant discussion. If today the participation of the ancient Churches of the East, the younger Churches in Asia and Africa, and the Roman Catholic Church in the dialogue has complicated the issue and multiplied the problems, it is at the same time an indication of the vitality of the movement.

Important as are the theological discussions at present taking place, the implications of a true ecumenism extend beyond the boundaries of such debate. With innumerable opportunities for active collaboration in many areas of social life at hand, cooperation between Christians cannot await dogmatic agreement between Christians. Thus, as the present Archbishop of Canterbury suggested in a notable interview in the *Catholic Herald*, much could be done immediately to commend Christianity to the world through a united defence of basic religious and moral beliefs. Many, for example, who have watched the development of our affluent society, as it is called, have wondered if it does not create as many problems as it solves. From all indications, it is likely that it will become ever more affluent in the future with serious consequences for man who will need a new kind of vigour to resist degeneration and the corrupting influence of wealth and luxury. Through the bitter experience of the past, the dehumanizing effects of penury and want are known; now the dehumanizing effects of wealth and affluence must be studied. It would be no small service to society and to the human race if the various Christian communions would lend their combined weight and sanction to this problem and its solution. The practice of a certain asceticism in the midst of affluence and the inculcation of habits of personal restraint and outward-looking unselfishness would benefit from the witness of a freely united, world-wide Christian community. Surely the resources at hand are adequate to meet this special human emergency if we but call upon them.

The increase of leisure time is another development of the years ahead fraught with implications of importance for all serious-minded men. A further shortening of the working day and working week seems likely, adding new hours to relaxation and leisure which were formerly taken up with crushing labour. The question of whether in fact these new-found hours will be filled with creative activities which realize the high potential of the human personality must be faced. The frivolous nature of so much of our present socializing, the mediocrity of mass entertainment, and the excessive seeking after excitement which characterize so much of the recreational and leisure time activities of our times do not offer much hope. Yet Christians cannot afford to neglect the plight of man at his ease, for of what use to escape the slavery of labour only to be trapped in the numbing slavery of indolence.

While it can readily be granted that many features of the welfare state have profoundly Christian implications, it must also be admitted that these can easily be lost in a sea of bureaucratic controls. Charity is not indeed a substitute for justice, nevertheless its role is more, not less, important in the complex pattern of our present society which can seem to reduce the person to a unit of administration. Here again a common sense of urgency in the face of this threat to Christian values could prove very productive.

If the Church has learned anything from the contemporary world, it is that it is virtually impossible to separate its spiritual mission from the temporal, social, and political welfare of man. Fortunately, the Church in the English-speaking world has managed to establish a fairly good reputation in the matter of social justice. This accounts in large part for its success in holding the great body of its working class adherents, in happy contrast to the tragic loss of them which marked the history of the Church in nineteenth-century Europe. The lamentable exception to this, however, is the

Catholic record in the matter of racial equality in the United States.

In an earlier chapter the reasons why the American Church failed to gain a large Negro following after the Civil War were touched upon. For many decades thereafter, the Church passively accepted the prevailing mores which by segregation forced the Negro into a servile and degrading place in American society. It is true that from time to time individual bishops spoke out against racial injustice, but without effecting any substantial change in the prevailing Catholic practice particularly in the South. In 1947, however, seven years before the 1954 judgement of the Supreme Court, Archbishop Joseph E. Ritter of St Louis moved to end segregation in the schools of his archdiocese. Since that time Catholics have been taking a noteworthy rôle in pressing for racial justice.

The Church's official utterances have been clear and emphatic, and the collective statement of the American hierarchy in 1958 on Negro rights showed no hesitation in speaking of the sin of segregation. This condemnation of racism has since been spelled out in ever sharper detail, in words and deeds by bishops in all parts of the United States. In a pastoral letter of March, 1963, Archbishop Lawrence J. Shehan of Baltimore called on Catholics in "the oldest and most venerable See in the United States" to put an end to discrimination, not allowing prudence "to serve as an excuse for inaction or unnecessary gradualism". The archbishop made it plain that in churches and parochial life generally there must be, not only no racial segregation, but also no distinction of rank or place or treatment based on racial differences. "With humility and regret," Archbishop Shehan went on, "we Catholics must acknowledge that we have been all too slow in the correction of our shortcomings". This, he said, should lead us to "place ourselves in the forefront of movements to remove the injustices and discriminations which still remain."

Following the assassination in Jackson, Mississippi, in

June 1963, of Medger W. Evers, field secretary of the National Association for the Advancement of Colored People, Bishop Richard O. Gerow of the Diocese of Natchez-Jackson called upon all the people of Mississippi to face up to the moral problem of which the crime was a tragic symptom. Positive steps, he said, should be taken "toward recognizing the legitimate grievances of the Negro population". Bishop Victor J. Reed of Oklahoma City and Tulsa came out in support of "the validity and essential rightness of the massive acts of protest which have developed in response to continued injustices and practices of racial discrimination in American life."

Perhaps the most noteworthy instance to date was the letter which Cardinal Spellman directed to be read to Catholics of the great Archdiocese of New York, supporting the idea of peaceful demonstrations carried out in a spirit of "Christian charity and justice," and urging Catholic support of the August 28th, 1963 "March on Washington for Freedom and Jobs." Whether or not this late summer mass move on the nation's capital, which climaxed the series of demonstrations that exploded like sunbursts in many states across the country during the preceding months, will ever achieve its purpose of persuading the Congress to pass an effective civil rights programme remains to be seen. Whatever the result the fact remains that legislation alone, no matter how sweeping, cannot guarantee Negroes the meaningful participation in community life which is their right. The need at this moment —a full one hundred years after the Emancipation Proclamation—is for an aroused public conscience to eradicate discrimination in all its forms from American life. And in this task Christians cannot remain uncommitted.

The epoch of Church history which began when John XXIII gave the ecumenical movement a new dimension has already changed the face of Christendom. The rapprochement and understanding between Roman and non-Roman Christians, and the growing hunger for unity and brotherhood among men generally, will undoubtedly have its impact on the life of the Church and of the world for centuries to come. Moreover, the clearly discernible desire on the part of Christians to hasten their own reunion so that they may embark more effectively on the search for a core of unity for the human race is authentically Christian in inspiration. When death ended the pontificate of Pope John on June 3rd, 1963, the grief and sense of loss which welled up around the world was unprecedented—a modern miracle testifying to the fact that all varieties of men do indeed belong to one human family. The tributes paid to his memory came from men of every faith and no faith, proving that the enmities and divisions of mankind are not the whole reality of the human condition. The overwhelming effect of his short pontificate of less than five years was a unique thing in the Church. It gave to the world not merely a lovable and loving figure, a pontiff who mingled with the people, but a man of vision who by his two great encyclicals, *Mater et Magister* and *Pacem in Terris*, and by calling together the Ecumenical Council opened a new era in the life of the Church.

If one may anticipate the judgement of history, it would appear that the forces set in motion by Vatican Council II are irreversible. There is every reason to believe that they will be dominant in the reign of Pope Paul VI whose first address signalized the task of the Council as "the principal labour on which we intend to expend all the energies that the Lord has given us". The new pope further pledged himself "to pursue with every commitment" the great work begun by John XXIII and the goal that "all may be one". One may take hope, also, from the fact that Anglo-American Catholicism seems to be shedding, with its immigrant origins, that pronounced conservatism in matters of Church policy and religious renewal which has kept it lagging behind continental developments for so long, and to be struggling towards a Christian witness which is at once more mature, more demanding, and more inquiring.

SELECT BIBLIOGRAPHY

In this series: CRISTIANI, L.: *The Revolt against the Church;* GUILLEMAIN, Bernard: *The Early Middle Ages; The Later Middle Ages;* PALANQUE, Jean-Rémy: *The Church and the Dark Ages;* ZEILLER, Jacques: *Christian Beginnings.*

BECK, G. A. (Editor): *The English Catholics 1850-1950,* London, Burns and Oates, 1950.

BELLESHEIM, A.: *History of the Catholic Church in Scotland,* two volumes, Edinburgh, Blackwood, 1887-90.

BRENNAN, M. J.: *The Ecclesiastical History of Ireland,* Dublin, Duffy, 1864.

BROWN, W. E.: *The Catholic Church in South Africa,* edited by M. Derrick, London, Burns and Oates, and New York, Kenedy, 1960.

BURTON, E. H.: *The Life and Times of Bishop Challoner,* two volumes, London, Longmans, 1909.

BUTLER, E. C.: *The Life and Times of Bishop Ullathorne,* two volumes, London, Burns and Oates, 1926.

CALLAHAN, D.: *The Mind of the Catholic Layman,* New York, Scribners, 1963.

CURTAYNE, A.: *The Irish Story,* New York, Kenedy, 1960.

DAVIES, J. E.: *Catholicism in Medieval Wales,* London, Washbourne, 1916.

DEALY, M. B.: *Catholic Schools in Scotland,* Washington, D.C., Catholic University Press, 1945.

ELLIS, J. T.: *American Catholicism,* Chicago, University of Chicago Press, 1956; *Perspectives in American Catholicism,* Baltimore, Helicon, 1963; *The Life of James Cardinal Gibbons,* two volumes, Milwaukee, Bruce, 1952.

EVENNETT, H. O.: *The Catholic Schools of England and Wales,* Cambridge, Cambridge University Press, 1944.

FOGARTY, R.: *Catholic Education in Australia, 1806-1950,* two volumes, Melbourne, Melbourne University Press, 1959.

GALLAGHER, A. M.: *Education in Ireland,* Washington, D.C., Catholic University Press, 1948.

GWYNN, D. R.: *A Hundred Years of Catholic Emancipation 1829-1929,* London, Longmans, 1929.

HALES, E. E. Y.: *The Catholic Church in the Modern World,* London, Eyre and Spottiswoode, and New York, Hanover, 1958.

HUGHES, P.: *A History of the Church,* three volumes, London and New York, Sheed and Ward, 1934-47; *A Popular History of the Catholic Church,* London, Burns and Oates, and New York, Macmillan, 1951; *A Popular History of the Reformation,* London, Burns and Oates, and New York, Hanover, 1957; *The Catholic Question,* London, Sheed and Ward, 1929.

LALLY, F. J.: *The Catholic Church in a Changing America,* Boston, Little, Brown, 1962.

LATOURETTE, K. S.: *Christianity in a Revolutionary Age,* five volumes, London, Eyre and Spottiswoode, and New York, Harper, 1958-62; *History of the Expansion of Christianity,* seven volumes, London, Eyre and Spottiswoode, and New York, Harper, 1939-45.

LEYS, M. D. R.: *Catholicism in England,* 1559-1829, London, Longmans, 1961, and New York, Sheed and Ward, 1962.

McAVOY, T.: *Roman Catholicism and the American Way of Life,* Notre Dame, Ind., University of Notre Dame Press, 1960.

MACKENZIE, C.: *Catholicism and Scotland,* London, Routledge, 1936.

MATHEW, D.: *Catholicism in England 1535-1935,* London, Eyre and Spottiswoode, 3rd edn, 1955.

MAYNARD, T.: *Story of American Catholicism,* New York, Macmillan, 1941.

MELVILLE, A. M.: *John Carroll of Baltimore,* New York, Scribners, 1955.

MORAN, P. F.: *History of the Catholic Church in Australasia,* Sydney, Oceanic, 1894.

MURTAGH, J. G.: *Australia: The Catholic Chapter,* New York, Sheed and Ward, 1946.

O'BRIEN, E. M.: *The Foundation of Australia 1786-1800,* rev. edn, Sydney, Angus and Robertson, 1950; *The Dawn of*

Catholicism in Australia, two volumes, Sydney, Angus and Robertson, 1928.

ROEMER, T.: *The Catholic Church in the U.S.,* St. Louis, Herder, 1950.

SACKS, B.: *The Religious Issue in the State Schools of England and Wales,* 1902-14, Albuquerque, University of New Mexico Press, 1961.

SAINT-DENIS, D.: *The Catholic Church in Canada,* 6th edn, Montreal, Capuchin Convent, 1956.

SCOTT-MONCRIEFF, G.: *The Mirror and the Cross: Scotland and the Catholic Faith,* London, Burns and Oates, and Baltimore, Helicon, 1960.

TREVOR, M.: *Newman: The Pillar of the Cloud,* London, Macmillan, and New York, Doubleday, 1962; *Newman: Light in Winter,* London, Macmillan, 1962, and New York, Doubleday, 1963.

WALSH, P. J.: *William J. Walsh, Archbishop of Dublin,* Dublin, Longmans, 1928.

WARD, B. N.: *The Dawn of the Catholic Revival in England,* two volumes, London, Longmans, 1909; *The Eve of Catholic Emancipation,* three volumes, London, Longmans, 1911-12; *The Sequel to Catholic Emancipation,* two volumes, London, Longmans, 1915.

WATKIN, E. I.: *Roman Catholicism in England from the Reformation to 1950,* London, Oxford University Press, 1957.

WILLIAMSON, H. R.: *The Flowering Hawthorn,* New York, Hawthorn Books, 1962.